Intro to SQL: Everything You Need to Know to Build Databases

A Step-by-Step Guide to Mastering SQL Queries and Database Design

MIGUEL FARMER

RAFAEL SANDERS

Table of Content

TABLE OF CONTENTS

INTRODUCTION

Intro to SQL: Everything You Need to Know to Build Databases

In today's data-driven world, SQL (Structured Query Language) is the backbone of many systems, from small applications to massive enterprise-level databases. Whether you're a budding software developer, an aspiring data analyst, or simply someone eager to understand how the vast world of databases operates, SQL is an essential tool that every tech enthusiast needs to grasp.

But let's face it—SQL can feel daunting at first glance. There are numerous commands, clauses, functions, and concepts to learn. For beginners, the syntax may seem confusing, and for experts, the challenge often lies in optimizing performance and designing robust, scalable systems. That's where this book comes in.

Intro to SQL: Everything You Need to Know to Build Databases is designed to guide you through SQL in a clear, approachable way, providing both foundational knowledge and advanced techniques. It's built to cater to everyone—

from absolute beginners to seasoned professionals who want to refine their skills or refresh their knowledge.

A Clear, Structured Approach to Learning

SQL might seem complex, but with the right structure, anyone can master it. This book breaks down the key concepts of SQL in 27 chapters, each one building upon the previous, starting with the fundamentals and progressing to more sophisticated topics. The structure of the book is carefully curated to ensure that no topic is too overwhelming while still covering the full breadth of SQL capabilities.

For beginners, the early chapters will guide you through installing a database, understanding the syntax, and crafting your first SQL queries. As we move forward, you'll learn how to manipulate data, design databases, and optimize your queries for performance. Each chapter includes practical, real-world examples that help you apply what you've learned immediately. By the time you reach the final chapters, you'll have a solid understanding of advanced SQL techniques, including subqueries, triggers, stored procedures, and the finer points of database security and optimization.

For more experienced users, the book delves into more advanced topics that refine your knowledge and expand your expertise. You'll gain insights into performance optimization, advanced querying techniques, and practical database design principles that are essential for building large-scale applications. Even experienced developers will find value in the in-depth discussions of database architecture, security, and design best practices.

Why SQL? Why Now?

SQL is not just for database administrators or back-end developers. It's a universal language in the tech world, essential for anyone who works with data. Data is everywhere—from e-commerce transactions to social media interactions to scientific research—and SQL is the key to unlocking its potential.

Mastering SQL opens up a world of opportunities. Whether you're working with relational databases or just analyzing data stored in a database, SQL is your tool for extracting, updating, and manipulating data to answer real-world business or research questions. Whether you're building an application, running data queries for analysis, or simply managing your organization's data, SQL is the industry-standard tool that you cannot afford to overlook.

Real-World Application and Examples

One of the key aspects of this book is the emphasis on real-world examples. Every concept, from basic SELECT statements to complex subqueries and transaction management, is demonstrated using practical examples. These examples are drawn from real industries, including e-commerce platforms, social media, financial systems, and analytics applications. This will not only help you understand the theory but also show you how to apply these concepts in your daily work.

You'll also find hands-on exercises at the end of each chapter to ensure that you are actively practicing and solidifying what you've learned. From crafting simple queries to managing complex database systems, these exercises allow you to apply theory to practice in a meaningful way.

Database Design and Optimization

As you progress through the book, you'll see that SQL is not just about writing queries. It's about designing databases that are efficient, scalable, and maintainable. Early chapters introduce you to the basic concepts of database design, while later chapters dive into optimization techniques and performance tuning to help you build systems that can handle large datasets without slowing down.

Understanding indexing, normalization, and database security are key to ensuring that your systems are not only functional but also reliable and performant. This book will equip you with the skills to design efficient databases, optimize complex queries, and ensure that your systems are secure from malicious threats and vulnerabilities.

SQL in the Real World

While this book takes you through the syntax and concepts of SQL, it also emphasizes practical, real-world applications. We'll explore how SQL plays a vital role in industries like banking, healthcare, and e-commerce. You'll see how companies use SQL for tasks like data analysis, reporting, and business intelligence. By the time you're finished, you'll have a comprehensive understanding of how to build, manage, and query databases that are used in real-world applications.

13

A Journey for All Skill Levels

Whether you're just starting with SQL or looking to level up your existing knowledge, this book is designed to meet you where you are. Each chapter presents concepts in a clear, approachable manner with plenty of examples to ensure you stay engaged. As you progress, you'll encounter more advanced topics that are often glossed over in other resources. These insights will help you deepen your understanding of SQL and make you a more capable and confident database professional.

What You'll Learn

By the end of this book, you'll be able to:

- Understand SQL's role in database management and data retrieval
- Write basic to complex queries to extract and manipulate data
- Create and manage relational databases, tables, and indexes
- Optimize SQL queries for better performance
- Implement advanced techniques like stored procedures, triggers, and subqueries

- Design databases that are scalable, efficient, and secure
- Understand the future of SQL and database technologies

No matter your starting point, this book will provide you with the knowledge, confidence, and skills to excel in SQL and database management.

So, let's get started. The world of SQL is vast, but with this step-by-step guide, you'll master it in no time.

CHAPTER 1

WHAT IS SQL?

Purpose of SQL: Why It's Essential for Database Management

SQL, or **Structured Query Language**, is the standard language used for managing and manipulating relational databases. Think of it as the bridge between humans and databases. Without SQL, managing large amounts of structured data would be incredibly tedious, if not impossible. It provides a way to query, update, and interact with the data stored in a relational database, making it indispensable for tasks like retrieving customer records, processing transactions, or analyzing large datasets.

Databases, whether for a small business or a massive corporation, rely on SQL to efficiently organize, update, and retrieve data. SQL allows us to:

- **Query data**: SQL helps extract specific data from large datasets with just a few simple commands.
- **Insert, update, or delete data**: With SQL, you can manipulate data stored in tables, adding new records or changing existing ones.
- **Define the structure of data**: SQL allows you to create and modify tables, define relationships between them, and ensure data integrity.

16

- **Ensure data integrity**: Through constraints (such as primary keys and foreign keys), SQL ensures that data remains consistent and accurate.

Without SQL, accessing and working with databases would be much more complicated and less efficient. It's the language that empowers you to manage and interact with data in a structured and organized way.

Overview of Relational Databases: Basic Principles Behind Them

To understand how SQL works, it's crucial to first grasp the concept of **relational databases**, since SQL is designed specifically to interact with this type of database.

A **relational database** organizes data into tables, which are essentially grids or matrices consisting of rows and columns. These tables can be related to one another through shared attributes (often called **keys**). The relational model was introduced by **E.F. Codd** in the 1970s, and it forms the basis of how databases are structured today.

Here are a few key principles behind relational databases:

- **Tables**: Data is stored in tables (also called **relations**). Each table contains rows (also known as **records** or **tuples**) and columns (known as **attributes** or **fields**).

- o **Example**: A "Customers" table may have columns like `CustomerID`, `FirstName`, `LastName`, and `Email`.
- **Primary Keys**: Every table has a **primary key**, a unique identifier for each record. This ensures that each record in a table can be uniquely identified.
  - o **Example**: The `CustomerID` column in a "Customers" table would be the primary key, ensuring that each customer is uniquely identifiable.
- **Foreign Keys**: Foreign keys are used to link one table to another. They are columns that hold values from another table's primary key.
  - o **Example**: A "Orders" table might have a `CustomerID` column that links to the `CustomerID` in the "Customers" table, establishing a relationship between orders and customers.
- **Relationships**: The power of relational databases comes from the ability to create relationships between tables. These relationships can be one-to-one, one-to-many, or many-to-many, allowing for more complex data structures.
  - o **Example**: A "Customer" can place many "Orders", so there is a one-to-many relationship between the "Customers" and "Orders" tables.

18

Relational databases are ideal for organizing structured data that fits neatly into tables, with clear relationships between those tables. SQL helps manage these relationships by allowing you to join tables, filter data, and ensure referential integrity (the correctness of relationships between tables).

How SQL Works with Databases: The Connection Between Queries and Data Retrieval

SQL serves as the intermediary between the user (or application) and the relational database. It allows us to interact with the database by issuing commands, called **queries**, that request specific operations on the data. Here's a breakdown of how SQL interacts with databases:

1. **Database Structure**: First, a relational database is set up with one or more tables. These tables are designed to hold data in a structured format with specific columns, each corresponding to an attribute of the entity the table represents.

2. **Writing Queries**: Once the database is established, SQL queries are written to interact with that data. The most common SQL operations include:
   - **SELECT**: To retrieve data from a table.
   - **INSERT**: To add new data.
   - **UPDATE**: To modify existing data.
   - **DELETE**: To remove data.

3. **Query Processing**: When you issue a query, SQL passes it to the **database management system** (DBMS), which processes it. The DBMS determines how to retrieve the data and performs any necessary actions (like searching, sorting, or filtering).

    o   For instance, when you execute a `SELECT` query, SQL tells the DBMS, "Retrieve the data from this table and return it to me." The DBMS then checks the structure of the table, applies any necessary filters (based on the query), and returns the result.

4. **Execution**: Once the query is executed, the results are returned. For a `SELECT` query, this means the data that matches the query criteria will be displayed to the user or application. For other commands like `INSERT`, `UPDATE`, or `DELETE`, the database will reflect those changes immediately, based on the commands issued.

    o   **Example**: A `SELECT * FROM Customers WHERE City = 'New York';` command will instruct SQL to return all customers who live in New York from the "Customers" table.

SQL is essential because it allows users to directly manipulate, query, and retrieve data from the database in a way that's both efficient and reliable. It abstracts the complexities of interacting with raw data storage systems and provides a user-friendly, structured approach to data manipulation.

Conclusion

SQL is the backbone of relational database management systems, making it possible to efficiently store, manage, and retrieve data. In this chapter, we've covered the purpose of SQL, the basics of relational databases, and how SQL interacts with those databases to manage and manipulate data. As we continue through the book, you'll build on this foundation, learning how to work with SQL in practical ways, from querying data to optimizing database performance.

CHAPTER 2

SETTING UP YOUR ENVIRONMENT

In order to start using SQL, you first need to set up a working environment. Whether you're working locally on your computer or in a cloud-based environment, setting up your database system is crucial. This chapter will guide you through the process of installing popular SQL databases, connecting to them, and choosing the right tools for managing and interacting with your databases. By the end of this chapter, you'll be ready to write and execute SQL queries on a functional database system.

Installing SQL Databases: MySQL, PostgreSQL, SQLite, and Others

There are many SQL databases available, and choosing the right one depends on the nature of your project, your requirements for scalability, and the environment you're working in. Below, we'll cover how to install some of the most popular SQL database management systems (DBMS): MySQL, PostgreSQL, and SQLite. Each of these systems has unique features, and you can use any of them depending on your needs.

22

1. Installing MySQL

MySQL is one of the most widely used relational database systems. It's open-source, reliable, and scalable, often used in web applications.

Installation Steps:

- **For Windows:**
    1. Download the MySQL Installer from MySQL's official website.
    2. Run the installer and select the **MySQL Server** option.
    3. Follow the on-screen prompts, selecting the default configuration settings.
    4. Set a root password for the MySQL server (make sure to remember this!).
    5. Once installation is complete, MySQL will be ready for use.
- **For macOS:**
    1. Download the **MySQL Community Server** from MySQL Downloads.
    2. Open the downloaded file and follow the installation instructions.
    3. After installation, start the MySQL server by opening the **System Preferences** and selecting MySQL.

4. Use the **Terminal** to start and stop the server as needed.

- **For Linux (Ubuntu/Debian):**

  1. Open the terminal and run the following commands:

  ```bash

  sudo apt update
  sudo apt install mysql-server
  sudo mysql_secure_installation
  ```

  2. Follow the prompts to secure the MySQL installation and set the root password.

2. Installing PostgreSQL

PostgreSQL is an advanced open-source database system, known for its flexibility and support for complex queries. It's a great option for enterprise applications and large-scale systems.

Installation Steps:

- **For Windows:**

  1. Download the PostgreSQL installer from PostgreSQL's official website.

2. Run the installer and follow the prompts. Set a password for the PostgreSQL superuser (`postgres`).

3. Once installed, you can access PostgreSQL using the **pgAdmin** tool or through the **psql** command line interface.

- **For macOS:**

    1. Use **Homebrew** to install PostgreSQL by running the following commands in the terminal:

    ```bash

    brew install postgresql
    ```

    2. After installation, start the PostgreSQL service:

    ```bash

    brew services start postgresql
    ```

- **For Linux (Ubuntu/Debian):**

    1. Open the terminal and run the following commands:

    ```bash

    sudo apt update
    sudo apt install postgresql postgresql-contrib
    ```

25

```
sudo -i -u postgres
psql
```

3. Installing SQLite

SQLite is a lightweight, serverless SQL database that stores everything in a single file. It's a great choice for smaller applications, testing, or when you need a database that doesn't require a full-fledged server.

Installation Steps:

- **For Windows:**
    1. Download the SQLite installer from SQLite's official website.
    2. Extract the files to a directory, then open the command prompt to use the SQLite command line.
- **For macOS and Linux:**
    1. SQLite comes pre-installed on most macOS and Linux systems. You can check by running `sqlite3` in the terminal. If it's not installed, you can install it using Homebrew (for macOS) or apt (for Linux):
        - For macOS:

```
bash
```

```
brew install sqlite
```

26

- For Linux:

```bash

sudo apt install sqlite3
```

Connecting to a Database: Basic Setup for Using SQL in Local or Cloud Environments

Once you've installed a database, you need to connect to it. Connecting to your database can be done locally (on your own machine) or remotely (on a cloud-based server). Below, we'll discuss how to connect to a local and cloud-based database.

1. Connecting to a Local Database

For local databases like MySQL or PostgreSQL, the process is straightforward:

- **MySQL**:
    1. Open a terminal or command prompt.
    2. Run the following command to log into MySQL:

```bash

mysql -u root -p
```

    3. Enter your root password when prompted.

- **PostgreSQL**:
  1. Open a terminal.
  2. Run the following command to connect to the PostgreSQL database:

  ```bash

  psql -U postgres
  ```

- **SQLite**:
  1. Open a terminal.
  2. Navigate to the folder where the SQLite file is stored.
  3. Run the following command to open the SQLite shell:

  ```bash

  sqlite3 mydatabase.db
  ```

2. Connecting to a Cloud Database

Many organizations use cloud-based databases for scalability and remote access. Popular cloud databases include Amazon RDS (for MySQL, PostgreSQL, etc.) and Google Cloud SQL.

To connect to a cloud database, you typically need:

- The **hostname** (or IP address) of the database server.

- The **port number** used to connect (for MySQL, it's usually 3306; for PostgreSQL, it's 5432).
- The **database name**.
- **User credentials** (username and password).

For example, to connect to a MySQL database on AWS RDS:

1. Open a terminal or command prompt.
2. Run:

```bash

mysql -h your-db-hostname -u your-username -p
```

3. Enter your password when prompted.

Choosing Your Tools: Overview of Database Management Tools

While you can always interact with a database through the command line, using a **Database Management Tool** (DBMS) makes the process easier and more efficient. These tools provide graphical interfaces that help you visualize your data, run queries, and manage databases with ease.

Here are some of the most popular DBMS tools:

1. MySQL Workbench

MySQL Workbench is a visual tool for database design, querying, and administration. It's an official MySQL product and is highly recommended for MySQL users.

- **Features**:
  - o Visual design of database schemas.
  - o SQL query editor with syntax highlighting and autocompletion.
  - o Database management features like backups, user administration, and performance monitoring.

2. DBeaver

DBeaver is a universal database tool that supports MySQL, PostgreSQL, SQLite, and many other database systems. It's an excellent choice if you work with multiple databases.

- **Features**:
  - o Intuitive user interface with support for multiple databases.
  - o SQL editor with advanced features like code formatting, autocompletion, and query execution plans.
  - o Ability to connect to cloud databases, manage data, and generate reports.

3. pgAdmin

pgAdmin is the official management tool for PostgreSQL. It provides a comprehensive graphical interface for managing PostgreSQL databases, including features for running SQL queries and visualizing schema.

- **Features**:
    - o Query tool for executing SQL commands.
    - o Visual tools for managing database objects (tables, views, functions).
    - o Support for database maintenance and monitoring.

4. SQL Server Management Studio (SSMS)

For users working with Microsoft SQL Server, **SQL Server Management Studio (SSMS)** is the go-to tool. It allows database administrators to manage, configure, and interact with SQL Server instances.

- **Features**:
    - o Full-fledged database management and monitoring tools.
    - o Visual query builder and SQL scripting environment.
    - o Server performance monitoring and tuning.

31

Conclusion

Setting up your SQL environment is the first step to mastering SQL. In this chapter, we've covered how to install some of the most popular database systems (MySQL, PostgreSQL, SQLite), how to connect to both local and cloud databases, and an overview of useful database management tools that make interacting with your databases easier. By the end of this chapter, you should be equipped with the knowledge to start writing and executing SQL queries in your chosen environment.

CHAPTER 3

BASIC SQL SYNTAX

In this chapter, we will explore the core syntax that makes up SQL queries. Understanding SQL syntax is essential because it dictates how we write queries, interact with databases, and retrieve or manipulate data. We will break down the fundamental components of SQL, starting with the basic structure of a query, how to use the `SELECT` statement to retrieve data, and the importance of semicolons and comments in SQL code.

The Structure of a Query: Keywords, Clauses, and How They Come Together

SQL queries are composed of a series of **keywords** and **clauses** that work together to perform a task. Each part of a query plays a specific role, and understanding this structure is the first step in learning SQL.

1. Keywords

Keywords are predefined words that have a specific meaning in SQL. These are the building blocks of SQL queries and are case-insensitive, meaning you can write them in uppercase or lowercase. However, it's common practice to write SQL keywords in uppercase to improve readability.

Examples of keywords:

- SELECT: Used to retrieve data from a database.
- FROM: Specifies the table from which to retrieve data.
- WHERE: Filters data based on a condition.
- ORDER BY: Sorts the results in a specific order.

2. Clauses

Clauses are parts of an SQL statement that perform a specific function. Each query is made up of one or more clauses, each performing a particular operation or specifying additional details.

Common clauses:

- **SELECT clause**: Specifies the columns to be retrieved.
- **FROM clause**: Specifies the table from which the data is to be selected.
- **WHERE clause**: Filters the rows returned based on a condition.
- **ORDER BY clause**: Sorts the result set in ascending or descending order.

3. Structure of a Simple Query

A basic SQL query structure follows this general pattern:

```sql
SELECT column1, column2, ...
FROM table_name
WHERE condition
ORDER BY column_name;
```

Here's a breakdown of each component:

- **SELECT**: This is the keyword that specifies which columns you want to retrieve.
- **FROM**: This indicates the table where the data will come from.
- **WHERE**: This is an optional clause used to filter records based on specific conditions.
- **ORDER BY**: This is also optional and is used to sort the data by one or more columns.

Example Query:

```sql
SELECT FirstName, LastName
FROM Employees
WHERE Department = 'Sales'
ORDER BY LastName;
```

This query retrieves the `FirstName` and `LastName` columns from the `Employees` table, filtering only those who work in the 'Sales' department and sorting the results by the `LastName` in ascending order.

SELECT Statement: Introduction to Querying Data

The `SELECT` statement is the most commonly used command in SQL. It is used to retrieve data from one or more tables. The `SELECT` statement allows you to specify the exact data you want to see, including which columns to include, filtering criteria, and sorting rules.

1. Basic SELECT Statement

The simplest form of a `SELECT` statement involves specifying the columns you want to retrieve from a table. If you want to select all columns, you can use the `*` wildcard.

- **Select specific columns**:

  ```sql

  SELECT column1, column2
  FROM table_name;
  ```

- **Select all columns**:

```sql
sql


SELECT *
FROM table_name;
```

Example: To retrieve all columns from the `Employees` table:

```sql
sql

SELECT *
FROM Employees;
```

2. Using WHERE Clause to Filter Results

The `WHERE` clause is used to filter records that meet a specific condition. This is especially useful when you want to narrow down the result set to only include relevant records.

Syntax:

```sql
sql


SELECT column1, column2
FROM table_name
WHERE condition;
```

Example: Retrieve all employees in the 'Sales' department:

```sql
sql

SELECT FirstName, LastName
```

37

```
FROM Employees
WHERE Department = 'Sales';
```

You can also use operators like =, >, <, !=, BETWEEN, LIKE, and more to define conditions in the WHERE clause.

3. Using Logical Operators in WHERE Clause

Sometimes, you'll need to use multiple conditions in the WHERE clause. Logical operators like AND, OR, and NOT allow you to combine multiple conditions.

Example: Retrieve employees from the 'Sales' department who are older than 30 years:

sql

```
SELECT FirstName, LastName, Age
FROM Employees
WHERE Department = 'Sales' AND Age > 30;
```

4. Using the ORDER BY Clause

The ORDER BY clause allows you to sort the results of your query in ascending or descending order based on one or more columns.

Syntax:

sql

```
SELECT column1, column2
FROM table_name
ORDER BY column1 [ASC|DESC];
```

- **ASC**: Sorts results in ascending order (default).
- **DESC**: Sorts results in descending order.

Example: Sort employees by their LastName in descending order:

sql

```
SELECT FirstName, LastName
FROM Employees
ORDER BY LastName DESC;
```

5. Using LIMIT or OFFSET (Optional)

If you're working with large datasets and only need a portion of the results, you can limit the number of rows returned by the query.

Syntax:

sql

```
SELECT column1, column2
FROM table_name
LIMIT number_of_rows;
```

Example: Retrieve the first 5 employees:

```sql
SELECT FirstName, LastName
FROM Employees
LIMIT 5;
```

Using Semicolons and Comments: Basic Syntax Rules and Formatting

1. Semicolons

A semicolon (;) is used to signify the end of an SQL statement. It is important to include semicolons when writing multiple SQL statements in a script or when interacting with a database that requires them.

In most SQL environments, if you're writing a single query, the semicolon may not be strictly necessary. However, it is good practice to always include a semicolon at the end of a statement, especially when working with multiple queries.

Example:

```sql
SELECT * FROM Employees;
```

2. Comments

Comments are an important feature in SQL as they allow you to leave notes or explanations about your code. These comments are ignored by the database engine when executing queries.

There are two types of comments in SQL:

- **Single-line comments**: These are created using two hyphens (--).
- **Multi-line comments**: These are enclosed within /* and */.

Single-line comment:

sql

```
-- This query retrieves all employees
SELECT * FROM Employees;
```

Multi-line comment:

sql

```
/*
This query retrieves all employees who work in
the Sales department
and sorts them by LastName in ascending order.
*/
```

41

```
SELECT FirstName, LastName
FROM Employees
WHERE Department = 'Sales'
ORDER BY LastName;
```

Using comments effectively can help make your SQL code more readable and maintainable, especially when working with complex queries or sharing code with others.

Conclusion

In this chapter, we've covered the basic structure of SQL queries, starting with the key components like keywords, clauses, and their roles in forming a complete query. We introduced the SELECT statement as the primary method for querying data and explored how to filter results with the WHERE clause, sort results with ORDER BY, and limit the output. Additionally, we highlighted the importance of semicolons and comments in SQL syntax, which help ensure that queries are formatted correctly and that your code remains understandable. Mastering these basic syntax rules is essential as you begin writing and executing your SQL queries.

CHAPTER 4

SQL DATA TYPES

Understanding data types is crucial when working with SQL databases. Data types define the kind of data that can be stored in a column, helping ensure data integrity and enabling efficient querying. In this chapter, we'll explore the most common data types in SQL, how to choose the appropriate data type for your needs, and how NULL values are handled in SQL.

Common Data Types: INT, VARCHAR, DATE, and More

SQL offers a variety of data types to store different kinds of data. Choosing the right data type is essential for optimizing storage, maintaining data integrity, and ensuring that your queries run efficiently.

1. Numeric Data Types

Numeric data types are used to store numbers, both integers and floating-point values.

- **INT** (or **INTEGER**): Used to store whole numbers. For example, a field representing a person's age would likely use the INT type.

43

  o **Example**: `age INT`

- **FLOAT** and **DOUBLE**: Used to store decimal numbers with varying levels of precision. `FLOAT` stores single-precision floating-point numbers, while `DOUBLE` stores double-precision.

  o **Example:** `price FLOAT`

- **DECIMAL** (or **NUMERIC**): Used for storing fixed-point numbers. It's ideal for representing values where precision is important, such as monetary amounts.

  o **Example**: `salary DECIMAL(10, 2)` — This would store up to 10 digits, with 2 digits after the decimal point.

2. String Data Types

String data types store text-based data. The two most common string types are `CHAR` and `VARCHAR`.

- **CHAR**: Fixed-length string. When you define a `CHAR` column, it reserves the specified number of characters for each value, padding with spaces if necessary.

  o **Example**: `gender CHAR(1)` — This would store a single character for gender, e.g., 'M' or 'F'.

- **VARCHAR** (Variable-length Character String): Used for storing strings with varying lengths. Unlike `CHAR`, `VARCHAR` only uses as much space as needed for each value.

- o **Example**: `first_name VARCHAR(50)` — This would store a first name up to 50 characters long.
- **TEXT**: A variable-length string used to store large amounts of text data, like articles or descriptions.
  - o **Example**: `bio TEXT`

3. Date and Time Data Types

SQL provides various date and time data types to handle date and time information, ensuring you can work with timestamps and time intervals accurately.

- **DATE**: Stores a date value (year, month, and day).
  - o **Example**: `birthdate DATE`
- **TIME**: Stores time values (hours, minutes, seconds).
  - o **Example**: `event_time TIME`
- **DATETIME** (or **TIMESTAMP**): Stores both date and time values, typically with a higher level of precision.
  - o **Example**: `created_at DATETIME`
- **YEAR**: Stores a year in a 4-digit format.
  - o **Example**: `year_of_birth YEAR`

4. Boolean Data Type

- **BOOLEAN** (or **BOOL**): Stores true or false values, typically represented as `1` (TRUE) and `0` (FALSE).
  - o **Example**: `is_active BOOLEAN`

45

5. Binary Data Types

These data types are used to store binary data, such as images or files.

- **BLOB** (Binary Large Object): Used to store large amounts of binary data, like files, images, or videos.
  - **Example**: `profile_picture BLOB`

Choosing the Right Data Type: How to Decide Based on Your Data

Selecting the correct data type is crucial for efficient data storage and retrieval. Choosing an inappropriate data type can lead to wasted space, poor performance, and potential data integrity issues.

Here are some guidelines for choosing the right data type:

1. Consider the Nature of Your Data

- **For numbers**: If you're dealing with whole numbers, `INT` is generally the right choice. For decimal or floating-point values, use `FLOAT`, `DOUBLE`, or `DECIMAL` depending on precision requirements.
- **For text**: If the data has a consistent length (e.g., state abbreviations like "NY"), use `CHAR`. If the text can vary

46

in length (e.g., names, addresses), then VARCHAR is a better choice.

- **For dates**: If you need to store a date, use DATE. If you need both the date and time, use DATETIME or TIMESTAMP.

2. Size Considerations

- Use INT for smaller integers and BIGINT for larger integers.
- Use VARCHAR when you're unsure about the length of the text, but don't exceed the practical limits. For larger chunks of text, TEXT might be more appropriate.
- Always be cautious of memory usage when choosing data types — for instance, VARCHAR(255) takes more space than VARCHAR(50).

3. Storage and Performance

Choosing the right data type can have a significant impact on performance. For instance, using VARCHAR instead of CHAR for variable-length text can save space, while using DECIMAL ensures more accurate calculations with financial data. Additionally, indexing is more efficient when smaller data types are used, so aim to choose the smallest data type that can handle your data.

4. Data Integrity and Constraints

Using the appropriate data type helps maintain data integrity. For example, a DATE type ensures that only valid date values can be inserted into a column, while an INT column ensures that no non-numeric values are stored.

Working with NULL Values: How NULLs Behave in SQL

In SQL, a NULL value represents the absence of data or a missing value. It is not the same as an empty string (' ') or a zero value; it indicates that the value is unknown, not applicable, or not yet provided.

1. Inserting NULL Values

You can explicitly insert a NULL value into a column if the column allows it. Some columns may have NOT NULL constraints, meaning they cannot contain NULL values.

Example:

sql

```
INSERT INTO Employees (FirstName, LastName,
Department, Salary)
VALUES ('John', 'Doe', 'Sales', NULL);
```

48

In this case, the `Salary` is not provided, so it is assigned a NULL value.

2. Checking for NULL

To check if a column contains a NULL value, you cannot use the = operator. Instead, use the IS NULL or IS NOT NULL condition in the WHERE clause.

Example: Retrieve employees who don't have a salary value:

sql

```
SELECT FirstName, LastName
FROM Employees
WHERE Salary IS NULL;
```

Example: Retrieve employees who have a salary value:

sql

```
SELECT FirstName, LastName
FROM Employees
WHERE Salary IS NOT NULL;
```

3. NULL Behavior in Comparisons

When performing comparisons in SQL, any operation involving NULL will result in a NULL value, which is treated as unknown. For example:

```
sql
```

```
SELECT *
FROM Employees
WHERE Salary > NULL;
```

This query will return no results because NULL cannot be compared with a value using standard operators.

4. Handling NULL with Functions

Many SQL functions allow you to handle NULL values, such as:

- **COALESCE()**: Returns the first non-NULL value in a list.

  ```
  sql
  ```

  ```
  SELECT COALESCE(Salary, 0) FROM Employees;
  ```

  This will return 0 if the Salary is NULL.

- **IFNULL()** (or NVL() in some databases): Similar to COALESCE(), it replaces NULL with a specified value.

  ```
  sql
  ```

  ```
  SELECT IFNULL(Salary, 0) FROM Employees;
  ```

5. NULLs and Aggregate Functions

Many aggregate functions (like SUM, AVG, COUNT, etc.) ignore NULL values by default. For instance, when calculating the average salary, NULL values are excluded from the calculation. However, you can customize this behavior using functions like COUNT(*) (which counts all rows, including those with NULL).

Conclusion

In this chapter, we covered the essential SQL data types, including numeric, string, date, and time types, as well as Boolean and binary data types. We also provided guidance on how to choose the right data type based on your data needs, and the importance of optimizing for storage, performance, and data integrity. Finally, we explored the behavior of NULL values in SQL, including how to insert, check, and handle them in queries. By understanding data types and NULL handling, you'll be able to build efficient and accurate SQL queries and maintain a clean and well-structured database.

CHAPTER 5

INTRODUCTION TO TABLES AND DATABASES

In this chapter, we'll introduce the fundamental concepts of **tables** and **databases** in SQL. Understanding how to create, modify, and organize tables is crucial for managing data effectively. We will cover how to create and modify tables, how to alter their structure when needed, and how databases are organized using tables, indexes, and schemas.

Creating and Modifying Tables: Syntax for Creating Tables

Tables are the fundamental building blocks of a database. They store the actual data in rows and columns, where each column holds a specific type of data (e.g., text, numbers, dates). In SQL, creating a table involves defining its structure, including the column names, data types, and constraints.

1. Creating a New Table

The basic syntax for creating a table is as follows:

```
sql
```

```
CREATE TABLE table_name (
    column1 datatype [constraint],
    column2 datatype [constraint],
    ...
);
```

Each column is defined by a **name** and a **data type**, with optional **constraints** such as NOT NULL, UNIQUE, or PRIMARY KEY.

Example:

Let's create a Customers table with columns for CustomerID, FirstName, LastName, Email, and DateOfBirth.

sql

```
CREATE TABLE Customers (
    CustomerID INT PRIMARY KEY,
    FirstName VARCHAR(50) NOT NULL,
    LastName VARCHAR(50) NOT NULL,
    Email VARCHAR(100) UNIQUE,
    DateOfBirth DATE
);
```

In this example:

- CustomerID is an INT and serves as the primary key, meaning it will uniquely identify each row in the table.

- `FirstName` and `LastName` are `VARCHAR` columns that cannot be `NULL`.
- `Email` is a `VARCHAR` column with a `UNIQUE` constraint to ensure no two customers have the same email.
- `DateOfBirth` is a `DATE` column to store the customer's birth date.

2. Defining Constraints

Constraints are rules that ensure the integrity of the data. Here are a few common constraints:

- **PRIMARY KEY**: Uniquely identifies each record in a table.
- **NOT NULL**: Ensures a column cannot contain a `NULL` value.
- **UNIQUE**: Ensures all values in a column are unique.
- **DEFAULT**: Assigns a default value if no value is specified.

Example (with a default value):

sql

```
CREATE TABLE Orders (
    OrderID INT PRIMARY KEY,
    OrderDate DATE DEFAULT CURRENT_DATE,
    CustomerID INT NOT NULL,
    TotalAmount DECIMAL(10, 2)
);
```

In this case, if no `OrderDate` is provided, the current date will be automatically assigned.

Altering Tables: Adding/Removing Columns, Changing Types

Once a table is created, you might need to modify it to accommodate new requirements. SQL provides several `ALTER TABLE` commands to modify the structure of an existing table, such as adding or removing columns, or changing the data type of a column.

1. Adding a New Column

To add a new column to an existing table, use the `ADD` keyword:

sql

```
ALTER TABLE table_name
ADD column_name datatype [constraint];
```

Example: Add a `PhoneNumber` column to the `Customers` table:

sql

```
ALTER TABLE Customers
ADD PhoneNumber VARCHAR(15);
```

2. Modifying an Existing Column

If you need to change the data type of an existing column, use the MODIFY keyword (in some databases like MySQL) or ALTER COLUMN (in databases like PostgreSQL).

Example (MySQL): Change the PhoneNumber column to allow a larger string:

sql

```
ALTER TABLE Customers
MODIFY PhoneNumber VARCHAR(25);
```

Example (PostgreSQL): In PostgreSQL, you would use ALTER COLUMN:

sql

```
ALTER TABLE Customers
ALTER COLUMN PhoneNumber TYPE VARCHAR(25);
```

3. Dropping (Removing) a Column

If a column is no longer needed, you can remove it using the DROP keyword:

sql

```
ALTER TABLE table_name
```

```
DROP COLUMN column_name;
```

Example: Remove the `PhoneNumber` column from the `Customers` table:

sql

```
ALTER TABLE Customers
DROP COLUMN PhoneNumber;
```

4. Renaming a Column

To rename a column, use the `RENAME COLUMN` command (syntax varies by database type):

Example (PostgreSQL):

sql

```
ALTER TABLE Customers
RENAME COLUMN PhoneNumber TO ContactNumber;
```

Example (MySQL):

sql

```
ALTER TABLE Customers
CHANGE COLUMN PhoneNumber ContactNumber
VARCHAR(15);
```

57

5. Renaming a Table

If you want to rename an entire table, you can use the RENAME TO command:

sql

```
ALTER TABLE old_table_name
RENAME TO new_table_name;
```

Example:

sql

```
ALTER TABLE Customers
RENAME TO Clients;
```

Database Structure: How Databases Are Organized with Tables, Indexes, and Schemas

Databases are not just collections of tables. They also have a structure that organizes and optimizes data access. Let's look at the components that make up the structure of a database.

1. Tables

Tables are where all the actual data is stored. A single database can contain multiple tables, each designed to store different types of data (e.g., Customers, Orders, Products).

2. Indexes

Indexes are used to speed up the retrieval of rows from a table. They function like indexes in a book, allowing the database engine to find data faster without scanning the entire table. Indexes are created on one or more columns of a table and help improve performance, especially with large datasets.

To create an index on a column, use the CREATE INDEX statement:

```sql
CREATE INDEX index_name
ON table_name (column_name);
```

Example: Create an index on the Email column of the Customers table:

```sql
CREATE INDEX idx_email
ON Customers (Email);
```

Indexes improve query performance for certain operations (like `SELECT`), but they can slow down data modification operations (like `INSERT`, `UPDATE`, `DELETE`). It's important to balance the need for fast queries with the overhead introduced by indexes.

3. Schemas

A schema is a collection of database objects, including tables, views, indexes, and constraints. Schemas help organize objects within a database. By default, when you create a table or other object, it is placed in the `public` schema (in PostgreSQL) or the default schema for the database.

You can create a schema and then create tables within it to better organize the database objects.

Example: Create a schema and a table within it:

sql

```sql
CREATE SCHEMA Sales;
CREATE TABLE Sales.Orders (
    OrderID INT PRIMARY KEY,
    CustomerID INT,
    OrderDate DATE
);
```

Schemas are particularly useful for large databases, where different departments or projects may need to have their own logical data structures while still being in the same physical database.

Conclusion

In this chapter, we introduced the core concepts of creating and modifying tables in SQL. We explored how to define tables, add new columns, modify existing ones, and remove unnecessary columns using the `ALTER TABLE` command. We also covered the structure of databases, including the use of indexes for improving query performance and schemas for better organization of database objects. With this foundational knowledge, you'll be able to effectively manage and modify your database structure to suit your needs.

CHAPTER 6

INSERTING DATA

In SQL, **inserting data** into tables is one of the most fundamental operations. This chapter will cover the basics of the INSERT statement, how to efficiently insert multiple records at once, and how to troubleshoot common errors that may arise during data insertion.

Basic INSERT Statement: How to Add Rows to Your Tables

The INSERT INTO statement is used to add new rows of data into an existing table. It is important to ensure that the data you are inserting matches the structure of the table, including the column order and data types.

1. Syntax for Inserting Data

The basic syntax for inserting a single row of data is:

```sql

INSERT    INTO    table_name    (column1,    column2,
column3, ...)
VALUES (value1, value2, value3, ...);
```

- `table_name`: The name of the table into which data is being inserted.
- `column1, column2, ...`: The columns in the table that you are inserting data into.
- `value1, value2, ...`: The values to be inserted into the respective columns.

Example:

Insert a new record into the `Customers` table:

sql

```
INSERT INTO Customers (CustomerID, FirstName,
LastName, Email, DateOfBirth)
VALUES        (1,         'John',        'Doe',
'john.doe@example.com', '1985-05-15');
```

In this example:

- `CustomerID` is an integer, and `FirstName`, `LastName`, `Email`, and `DateOfBirth` are provided as values that match the respective column data types.

2. Inserting Data Without Specifying Columns

If you're inserting data into **all** the columns of a table in the order they were defined, you don't need to specify the column names.

However, this is less common and can lead to errors if the table structure changes over time.

Example:

sql

```
INSERT INTO Customers
VALUES      (2,      'Jane',      'Smith',
'jane.smith@example.com', '1990-07-22');
```

This will insert a new row into the Customers table, assuming the values are in the same order as the columns.

3. Default Values

If a column has a default value (e.g., CURRENT_DATE for a date column), you can skip it in the INSERT statement.

Example:

sql

```
INSERT   INTO   Orders   (OrderID,   CustomerID,
TotalAmount)
VALUES (1, 2, 150.00);
```

Here, OrderDate would automatically be assigned the default value (CURRENT_DATE), as defined when the table was created.

Inserting Multiple Records: Efficient Data Insertion

Inserting multiple rows of data at once is a common task, especially when importing large datasets. SQL allows you to insert multiple records in a single INSERT INTO statement, which is more efficient than inserting each record individually.

1. Syntax for Inserting Multiple Rows

You can insert multiple rows by separating each set of values with a comma.

sql

```
INSERT INTO table_name (column1, column2,
column3, ...)
VALUES
    (value1a, value2a, value3a, ...),
    (value1b, value2b, value3b, ...),
    (value1c, value2c, value3c, ...);
```

Example:

sql

```
INSERT INTO Customers (CustomerID, FirstName,
LastName, Email, DateOfBirth)
VALUES
```

65

```
    (3,            'Alice',            'Johnson',
'alice.johnson@example.com', '1992-11-01'),
    (4, 'Bob', 'Brown', 'bob.brown@example.com',
'1988-02-19'),
    (5,            'Charlie',            'Davis',
'charlie.davis@example.com', '1995-08-30');
```

This statement inserts three rows into the Customers table in a single operation, making it more efficient than three separate INSERT statements.

2. Using SELECT for Bulk Insertion

You can also insert data into a table by selecting it from another table. This is especially useful when transferring data between tables or when performing transformations before inserting.

Example:

sql

```
INSERT  INTO  Customers  (CustomerID,  FirstName,
LastName, Email, DateOfBirth)
SELECT EmployeeID, FirstName, LastName, Email,
HireDate
FROM Employees;
```

In this example, data from the `Employees` table is inserted into the `Customers` table. The column values are mapped based on their position in both tables.

Handling Errors: How to Troubleshoot Common Insertion Problems

While inserting data into SQL tables is generally straightforward, several issues can arise. Below are some common errors and how to troubleshoot them.

1. Inserting Null Values in Non-Nullable Columns

One of the most common errors occurs when trying to insert a `NULL` value into a column that does not allow `NULL`s (i.e., a column with a `NOT NULL` constraint).

Error Example:

sql

```
INSERT INTO Customers (CustomerID, FirstName,
LastName, Email, DateOfBirth)
VALUES (6, 'David', 'Miller', NULL, '1990-12-
10');
```

If the `Email` column has a `NOT NULL` constraint, the above query will fail because `NULL` is being inserted into a non-nullable column.

Solution:

Make sure you provide a valid value for non-nullable columns. You can either update the data to meet the column's constraints or modify the table to allow `NULL` values in that column (if appropriate).

sql

```
ALTER TABLE Customers
MODIFY Email VARCHAR(100) NULL;
```

2. Mismatched Data Types

Another common issue is inserting a value that does not match the column's data type. For example, trying to insert a string into an `INT` column will cause an error.

Error Example:

sql

```
INSERT INTO Customers (CustomerID, FirstName,
LastName, Email, DateOfBirth)
VALUES ('ABC', 'Emma', 'Green',
'emma.green@example.com', '1992-09-20');
```

If CustomerID is an INT column, this statement will fail because 'ABC' is a string, not an integer.

Solution:

Ensure that the data types in the INSERT statement match the column definitions in the table. In the case above, CustomerID should be an integer, so you need to provide a valid integer value.

3. Violating Unique Constraints

If you try to insert a duplicate value into a column that is marked as UNIQUE (e.g., an email or user ID), SQL will throw a violation error.

Error Example:

sql

```
INSERT INTO Customers (CustomerID, FirstName,
LastName, Email, DateOfBirth)
VALUES      (7,      'Frank',      'Taylor',
'john.doe@example.com', '1980-03-25');
```

If the email 'john.doe@example.com' already exists in the Customers table, this insert will fail because Email is unique.

Solution:

Check for existing values before inserting or use INSERT IGNORE (in MySQL) or ON CONFLICT DO NOTHING (in PostgreSQL) to avoid errors when inserting duplicates.

Example in MySQL:

```sql
```

```sql
INSERT IGNORE INTO Customers (CustomerID,
FirstName, LastName, Email, DateOfBirth)
VALUES      (7,       'Frank',      'Taylor',
'john.doe@example.com', '1980-03-25');
```

4. Missing Columns in INSERT

If you forget to include a value for a column that does not have a default value and is marked NOT NULL, the insert will fail.

Error Example:

```sql
```

```sql
INSERT INTO Customers (CustomerID, FirstName,
LastName)
VALUES (8, 'Grace', 'Lee');
```

If the `Email` column is `NOT NULL` and does not have a default value, this statement will fail because no value is provided for the `Email` column.

Solution:

Make sure to provide values for all non-nullable columns, or modify the table to allow `NULL` values or set default values for columns that can be left empty.

Conclusion

In this chapter, we covered the core concepts of inserting data into SQL tables. We explored the basic `INSERT` statement syntax, inserting multiple records in a single operation, and how to efficiently bulk insert data using `SELECT`. We also examined common errors that occur during data insertion, such as violating constraints, mismatched data types, and inserting `NULL` values into non-nullable columns. By understanding these concepts and troubleshooting common errors, you'll be able to insert data efficiently and avoid pitfalls in your SQL operations.

CHAPTER 7

RETRIEVING DATA WITH SELECT

In SQL, retrieving data from a database is one of the most common tasks. The SELECT statement is used to query and retrieve data from one or more tables. In this chapter, we will cover the basics of the SELECT query, how to filter data using the WHERE clause, and how to sort data using the ORDER BY clause. These essential techniques will help you to retrieve exactly the data you need.

Basic SELECT Queries: Fetching Data from a Table

The SELECT statement is the core of SQL when it comes to retrieving data. It allows you to fetch data from a table, and you can specify which columns you want to retrieve. If you want to fetch all columns, you can use the wildcard * symbol.

1. Syntax for a Simple SELECT Query

The simplest form of a SELECT query retrieves all columns from a table:

sql

```
SELECT * FROM table_name;
```

- * is a wildcard that means "all columns."
- table_name is the name of the table you want to query.

Example:

sql

```
SELECT * FROM Customers;
```

This will retrieve all rows and columns from the Customers table.

2. Selecting Specific Columns

If you don't need all the columns, you can specify which columns to retrieve by listing them after SELECT.

sql

```
SELECT column1, column2, column3 FROM table_name;
```

Example:

sql

```
SELECT FirstName, LastName, Email FROM Customers;
```

This will only retrieve the `FirstName`, `LastName`, and `Email` columns from the `Customers` table.

3. Limiting the Number of Results

In many cases, you might want to limit the number of rows returned, especially when working with large datasets. You can use the `LIMIT` clause to restrict the number of rows returned.

Example:

sql

```
SELECT * FROM Customers
LIMIT 5;
```

This will retrieve the first 5 rows from the `Customers` table. Note that `LIMIT` is typically used in databases like MySQL and PostgreSQL, but for SQL Server, you would use `TOP`.

sql

```
SELECT TOP 5 * FROM Customers;
```

Filtering Data with WHERE: Using Conditions to Narrow Results

The `WHERE` clause is used to filter records based on a specified condition. Without `WHERE`, the `SELECT` query would return all rows from the table. The WHERE clause allows you to fetch only the rows that meet certain criteria.

1. Syntax for Using WHERE

sql

```
SELECT column1, column2, ...
FROM table_name
WHERE condition;
```

- condition: A condition that must be met for rows to be returned (e.g., equality, range, or pattern matching).

Example:

sql

```
SELECT FirstName, LastName, Email FROM Customers
WHERE CustomerID = 3;
```

This will retrieve the FirstName, LastName, and Email columns from the Customers table where the CustomerID is 3.

2. Using Comparison Operators

The WHERE clause allows you to filter rows based on comparison operators. Some common comparison operators include:

- = (equal)

75

- != or <> (not equal)
- > (greater than)
- < (less than)
- >= (greater than or equal to)
- <= (less than or equal to)

Example:

sql

```
SELECT * FROM Customers
WHERE DateOfBirth > '1990-01-01';
```

This will retrieve all customers whose DateOfBirth is later than January 1, 1990.

3. Using AND, OR, and NOT

You can combine multiple conditions using AND, OR, and NOT to create more complex filters.

- **AND**: Both conditions must be true.
- **OR**: At least one condition must be true.
- **NOT**: Reverses the condition (i.e., exclude rows that match the condition).

Example (AND):

sql

```
SELECT * FROM Customers
WHERE FirstName = 'John' AND LastName = 'Doe';
```

This retrieves all customers named "John Doe."

Example (OR):

```
sql
```

```
SELECT * FROM Customers
WHERE FirstName = 'John' OR FirstName = 'Alice';
```

This retrieves all customers named either "John" or "Alice."

Example (NOT):

```
sql
```

```
SELECT * FROM Customers
WHERE NOT FirstName = 'John';
```

This retrieves all customers whose first name is not "John."

4. Using LIKE for Pattern Matching

The LIKE operator allows you to search for patterns within text columns. You can use wildcard characters:

- %: Matches any sequence of characters (including an empty sequence).
- _: Matches a single character.

Example (wildcard with %):

sql

```
SELECT * FROM Customers
WHERE Email LIKE '%@example.com';
```

This retrieves all customers whose email addresses end with @example.com.

Example (wildcard with _):

sql

```
SELECT * FROM Customers
WHERE FirstName LIKE 'J_n';
```

This retrieves customers whose first name starts with "J" and ends with "n" (e.g., "John" or "Jan").

Sorting Data: Using ORDER BY to Sort Results

By default, SQL queries return rows in no particular order. To control the order of the result set, you can use the ORDER BY clause. The ORDER BY clause sorts the result set based on one or more columns.

1. Syntax for ORDER BY

sql

```
SELECT column1, column2, ...
FROM table_name
ORDER BY column1 [ASC|DESC];
```

- ASC: Sorts in ascending order (this is the default).
- DESC: Sorts in descending order.

2. Sorting by One Column

To sort by a single column, specify the column name in the ORDER BY clause:

Example (ascending order):

sql

```
SELECT * FROM Customers
ORDER BY LastName;
```

This will retrieve all customers, sorted by their last name in ascending order (alphabetically).

Example (descending order):

sql

```
SELECT * FROM Customers
ORDER BY LastName DESC;
```

This will retrieve all customers, sorted by their last name in descending order (Z to A).

3. Sorting by Multiple Columns

You can also sort by multiple columns. The rows will be sorted first by the first column, and if there are duplicates, they will be sorted by the second column, and so on.

Example (multi-column sort):

sql

```
SELECT * FROM Customers
ORDER BY LastName ASC, FirstName ASC;
```

This will sort the customers first by their last name, then by their first name (both in ascending order).

4. Sorting with NULL Values

In SQL, NULL values are sorted separately from other values, and the order in which they appear can vary depending on the database. Typically, NULL values are either sorted first (when using ASC) or last (when using DESC), but this can be controlled with NULLS FIRST or NULLS LAST in some SQL dialects.

Example (PostgreSQL):

sql

```
SELECT * FROM Customers
ORDER BY LastName ASC NULLS LAST;
```

This will sort customers by their last name in ascending order, placing any NULL values at the end.

Conclusion

In this chapter, we've covered how to use the SELECT statement to retrieve data from a table. We learned how to filter data with the WHERE clause using comparison operators, logical operators like AND, OR, and NOT, and pattern matching with LIKE. We also explored how to sort query results with ORDER BY, including sorting by multiple columns and handling NULL values. These are essential techniques for efficiently retrieving and manipulating data in SQL, and mastering them will enable you to perform powerful queries on your database.

CHAPTER 8

WORKING WITH OPERATORS AND EXPRESSIONS

In SQL, **operators** allow you to perform various types of operations on data, such as logical operations, comparisons, and mathematical calculations. Understanding how to work with these operators and expressions is essential for crafting powerful and precise queries. In this chapter, we will explore the main types of operators: **logical operators**, **comparison operators**, and **arithmetic operators**, and how to use them in SQL queries to manipulate and filter data.

Logical Operators: AND, OR, NOT

Logical operators are used to combine multiple conditions in a query's WHERE clause. They allow you to refine the criteria for selecting data by making sure multiple conditions are met simultaneously or separately. The three most commonly used logical operators are AND, OR, and NOT.

82

1. AND Operator

The AND operator allows you to combine multiple conditions, and only rows where **all** conditions are true will be returned.

Syntax:

```sql
SELECT column1, column2
FROM table_name
WHERE condition1 AND condition2;
```

Example:

```sql
SELECT * FROM Customers
WHERE FirstName = 'John' AND LastName = 'Doe';
```

This will return all customers whose first name is "John" and last name is "Doe."

2. OR Operator

The OR operator is used when you want to retrieve rows where **at least one** of the conditions is true. It provides more flexibility when you're interested in multiple conditions.

Syntax:

```
sql
```

```
SELECT column1, column2
FROM table_name
WHERE condition1 OR condition2;
```

Example:

```
sql
```

```
SELECT * FROM Customers
WHERE FirstName = 'John' OR FirstName = 'Alice';
```

This query returns customers whose first name is either "John" or "Alice."

3. NOT Operator

The NOT operator is used to exclude rows that match a specified condition. It reverses the result of the condition that follows it.

Syntax:

```
sql
```

```
SELECT column1, column2
FROM table_name
WHERE NOT condition;
```

Example:

```sql
sql
```

```sql
SELECT * FROM Customers
WHERE NOT FirstName = 'John';
```

This will return all customers whose first name is not "John."

Comparison Operators: =, <>, <, >, BETWEEN, LIKE, etc.

Comparison operators allow you to compare values and return rows that meet specific criteria. They are fundamental for filtering data based on conditions such as equality, range, and pattern matching.

1. Equal to (=)

The = operator is used to test for equality between two values.

Example:

```sql
sql
```

```sql
SELECT * FROM Customers
WHERE FirstName = 'John';
```

This query will return all customers whose first name is exactly "John."

2. Not Equal to (<> or !=)

The <> (or != in some SQL dialects) operator is used to test for inequality between two values. It returns rows where the condition is **not** true.

Example:

sql

```
SELECT * FROM Customers
WHERE FirstName <> 'John';
```

This will return all customers whose first name is not "John."

3. Less Than (<) and Greater Than (>)

The < and > operators are used to compare numeric or date values and return rows where the condition is true.

Example (Less Than):

sql

```
SELECT * FROM Orders
WHERE TotalAmount < 100;
```

This will return all orders where the total amount is less than 100.

Example (Greater Than):

```sql
sql
```

```sql
SELECT * FROM Orders
WHERE TotalAmount > 500;
```

This will return all orders where the total amount is greater than 500.

4. BETWEEN

The BETWEEN operator is used to filter results within a specific range. It can be used with numeric, date, or text values.

Syntax:

```sql
sql
```

```sql
SELECT column1, column2
FROM table_name
WHERE column_name BETWEEN value1 AND value2;
```

Example:

```sql
sql
```

```sql
SELECT * FROM Orders
WHERE OrderDate BETWEEN '2025-01-01' AND '2025-12-31';
```

This will return all orders placed in the year 2025.

5. LIKE

The LIKE operator is used to search for a specified pattern in a column. It is commonly used with wildcard characters:

- %: Matches zero or more characters.
- _: Matches exactly one character.

Example (Pattern Matching with %):

sql

```
SELECT * FROM Customers
WHERE Email LIKE '%@example.com';
```

This will return all customers whose email ends with @example.com.

Example (Pattern Matching with _):

sql

```
SELECT * FROM Customers
WHERE FirstName LIKE 'J_n';
```

This will return all customers whose first name starts with "J" and ends with "n" (e.g., "John" or "Jan").

6. IN

The IN operator allows you to check if a value matches any value in a list of values, making it a simpler alternative to using multiple OR conditions.

Example:

sql

```
SELECT * FROM Customers
WHERE FirstName IN ('John', 'Alice', 'Bob');
```

This will return customers whose first name is either "John," "Alice," or "Bob."

7. IS NULL / IS NOT NULL

The IS NULL operator is used to check whether a column contains a NULL value. The IS NOT NULL operator checks if the column does not contain NULL.

Example (IS NULL):

sql

```
SELECT * FROM Customers
WHERE Email IS NULL;
```

This will return all customers who do not have an email address.

Example (IS NOT NULL):

```sql
SELECT * FROM Customers
WHERE Email IS NOT NULL;
```

This will return all customers who have an email address.

Arithmetic Operators: Calculations and Mathematical Expressions in Queries

Arithmetic operators are used to perform mathematical calculations on numeric data. They allow you to create more complex queries that involve calculations, such as totals, averages, and percentage calculations.

1. Addition (+)

The + operator is used to add values.

Example:

```sql
```

```
SELECT ProductName, Price, Discount, Price +
Discount AS TotalPrice
FROM Products;
```

This will return a list of products along with their price, discount, and the total price (price + discount).

2. Subtraction (-)

The – operator is used to subtract values.

Example:

sql

```
SELECT ProductName, Price, SalePrice, Price -
SalePrice AS DiscountAmount
FROM Products;
```

This will return the discount amount for each product by subtracting the sale price from the original price.

3. Multiplication (*)

The * operator is used to multiply values.

Example:

sql

```
SELECT    ProductName,    Quantity,    UnitPrice,
Quantity * UnitPrice AS TotalCost
FROM OrderDetails;
```

This will return the total cost for each item in an order by multiplying the quantity by the unit price.

4. Division (/)

The / operator is used to divide values.

Example:

sql

```
SELECT    ProductName,    TotalAmount,    Quantity,
TotalAmount / Quantity AS UnitPrice
FROM Orders;
```

This will return the unit price for each product by dividing the total amount by the quantity.

5. Modulo (%)

The % operator is used to return the remainder of a division operation.

Example:

sql

```
SELECT ProductID, Quantity, Quantity % 2 AS
IsEven
FROM Products;
```

This will return whether the quantity is even or odd by calculating the remainder when divided by 2.

Conclusion

In this chapter, we've covered the essential SQL operators: logical operators (AND, OR, NOT), comparison operators (=, <>, BETWEEN, LIKE, etc.), and arithmetic operators for performing calculations. By mastering these operators, you will be able to create more complex and flexible queries, enabling you to filter and manipulate data efficiently. Understanding how to use operators and expressions properly is fundamental to becoming proficient in SQL and using it to handle real-world data management tasks.

CHAPTER 9

JOINING TABLES

One of the most powerful and essential features in SQL is the ability to combine data from multiple tables. In real-world databases, data is often split across different tables to avoid redundancy and to follow normalization principles. Joining tables allows you to combine related data from these tables based on a shared key or relationship. In this chapter, we will explore the different types of SQL joins: **INNER JOIN**, **LEFT JOIN**, **RIGHT JOIN**, **FULL JOIN**, and **SELF JOIN**. We will also discuss when and how to use them effectively.

INNER JOIN: Combining Rows from Two Tables Based on a Condition

The INNER JOIN is one of the most commonly used types of join. It combines rows from two tables based on a condition, returning only the rows where there is a match in both tables. If there is no match, the row is excluded from the result set.

1. Syntax for INNER JOIN

sql

```
SELECT columns
FROM table1
INNER JOIN table2
ON table1.column = table2.column;
```

- `table1.column` and `table2.column` should be the columns that have a logical relationship, typically a foreign key and primary key.

Example:

Consider two tables: `Customers` and `Orders`. Each order is placed by a customer, and the `CustomerID` column in `Orders` corresponds to the `CustomerID` in `Customers`. To fetch a list of customers and their orders:

sql

```
SELECT              Customers.CustomerID,
Customers.FirstName,         Orders.OrderID,
Orders.OrderDate
FROM Customers
INNER JOIN Orders
ON Customers.CustomerID = Orders.CustomerID;
```

This query will return the customer information and their associated orders. Only customers who have placed an order will be included in the result.

2. Key Points about INNER JOIN

- Only returns rows with matching values in both tables.
- If there is no match in the JOIN condition, those rows are excluded from the result.

LEFT JOIN (or LEFT OUTER JOIN): Returning All Rows from the Left Table

The LEFT JOIN (or LEFT OUTER JOIN) returns all rows from the left table, even if there is no match in the right table. If there is no matching row in the right table, the result will include NULL for columns from the right table.

1. Syntax for LEFT JOIN
sql

```
SELECT columns
FROM table1
LEFT JOIN table2
ON table1.column = table2.column;
```

- The left table is always the first one mentioned in the query.

Example:

Let's say you want to find all customers and their orders, but you also want to include customers who haven't placed any orders. You can use a LEFT JOIN:

sql

```
SELECT                      Customers.CustomerID,
Customers.FirstName,                Orders.OrderID,
Orders.OrderDate
FROM Customers
LEFT JOIN Orders
ON Customers.CustomerID = Orders.CustomerID;
```

This will return all customers, including those who have not placed any orders. For customers with no orders, the OrderID and OrderDate will be NULL.

2. Key Points about LEFT JOIN

- Returns all rows from the left table.
- If no matching rows exist in the right table, NULL values are returned for columns from the right table.

RIGHT JOIN (or RIGHT OUTER JOIN): Returning All Rows from the Right Table

The `RIGHT JOIN` (or `RIGHT OUTER JOIN`) is similar to the `LEFT JOIN`, but it returns all rows from the right table, even if there is no matching row in the left table. If there is no match in the left table, `NULL` values will be returned for columns from the left table.

1. Syntax for RIGHT JOIN
sql

```
SELECT columns
FROM table1
RIGHT JOIN table2
ON table1.column = table2.column;
```

- The right table is always the second one mentioned in the query.

Example:

Suppose you want to find all orders, including those that may not have a customer associated with them (although this would be rare, it could happen in cases of system errors). You would use a `RIGHT JOIN`:

sql

98

```
SELECT                     Customers.CustomerID,
Customers.FirstName,            Orders.OrderID,
Orders.OrderDate
FROM Customers
RIGHT JOIN Orders
ON Customers.CustomerID = Orders.CustomerID;
```

This will return all orders, including those that do not have a corresponding customer. For orders with no associated customer, the `CustomerID` and `FirstName` will be `NULL`.

2. Key Points about RIGHT JOIN

- Returns all rows from the right table.
- If no matching rows exist in the left table, `NULL` values are returned for columns from the left table.

FULL JOIN (or FULL OUTER JOIN): Returning All Rows from Both Tables

The `FULL JOIN` (or `FULL OUTER JOIN`) returns all rows when there is a match in either the left or the right table. If there is no match, the result will contain `NULL` for the missing side of the join.

1. Syntax for FULL JOIN

sql

```
SELECT columns
FROM table1
FULL JOIN table2
ON table1.column = table2.column;
```

- This type of join returns every row from both tables.

Example:

If you want to find all customers and all orders, including customers without orders and orders without customers (again, rare but possible), you would use a FULL JOIN:

sql

```
SELECT              Customers.CustomerID,
Customers.FirstName,         Orders.OrderID,
Orders.OrderDate
FROM Customers
FULL JOIN Orders
ON Customers.CustomerID = Orders.CustomerID;
```

This will return every customer, every order, and if there is no match between them, it will display NULL for the columns where data is missing.

2. Key Points about FULL JOIN

- Returns all rows from both tables.

100

- If a row in the left table does not have a match in the right table, the result will have NULL for the right table's columns, and vice versa.

SELF JOIN: Joining a Table with Itself

A SELF JOIN is a join where a table is joined with itself. This is useful when you have hierarchical data or want to compare rows within the same table. It requires giving the table two different aliases to differentiate between the two instances of the same table.

1. Syntax for SELF JOIN

sql

```
SELECT a.column1, b.column2
FROM table_name a, table_name b
WHERE a.column = b.column;
```

- In this example, a and b are aliases for the same table, allowing you to refer to the table twice.

Example:

Consider a table Employees where each employee has a ManagerID that points to another employee. To find the names

101

of employees and their managers, you could perform a `SELF JOIN`:

sql

```
SELECT      e.EmployeeName      AS      Employee,
m.EmployeeName AS Manager
FROM Employees e
LEFT JOIN Employees m
ON e.ManagerID = m.EmployeeID;
```

This will return a list of employees with their corresponding managers, using a `LEFT JOIN` so that employees without managers are also included.

2. Key Points about SELF JOIN

- A `SELF JOIN` is simply a normal join where the same table is used twice.
- Use aliases (`e`, `m`, etc.) to differentiate between the two instances of the same table.

Conclusion

In this chapter, we have covered the essential types of SQL joins: `INNER JOIN`, `LEFT JOIN`, `RIGHT JOIN`, `FULL JOIN`, and `SELF`

`JOIN`. Understanding these joins allows you to combine and manipulate data from multiple tables in a way that reflects the relationships between them. Whether you need to find matching rows, include unmatched rows from one or both tables, or join a table to itself, mastering SQL joins is a key skill for anyone working with relational databases. By using the appropriate type of join for your data, you can extract meaningful insights and perform complex queries efficiently.

CHAPTER 10

AGGREGATING DATA

Aggregation is a powerful concept in SQL that allows you to perform operations on sets of data rather than individual rows. By using aggregate functions, you can calculate summaries and statistics such as totals, averages, minimums, and maximums. In this chapter, we will explore how to use aggregate functions like COUNT, SUM, AVG, MIN, and MAX, and how to organize and filter aggregated data using the GROUP BY and HAVING clauses.

COUNT, SUM, AVG, MIN, MAX: How to Aggregate Data

SQL provides several built-in aggregate functions to perform common calculations on data.

1. COUNT: Counting Rows

The COUNT() function is used to return the number of rows that match a specified condition. It can count all rows or just rows that contain non-NULL values in a specific column.

Syntax:

```sql
sql
```

```
SELECT COUNT(column_name)
FROM table_name
WHERE condition;
```

Example:

To count the number of customers in the `Customers` table:

sql

```
SELECT COUNT(CustomerID)
FROM Customers;
```

This query will return the total number of customers.

You can also count all rows regardless of NULL values by using `COUNT(*)`:

sql

```
SELECT COUNT(*)
FROM Customers;
```

This will return the total number of rows in the `Customers` table, including any rows with NULL values in the specified column.

2. SUM: Summing Values

The SUM() function is used to calculate the total sum of a numeric column.

Syntax:

sql

```
SELECT SUM(column_name)
FROM table_name
WHERE condition;
```

Example:

To find the total order amount from the Orders table:

sql

```
SELECT SUM(TotalAmount)
FROM Orders;
```

This will return the total of the TotalAmount column for all orders.

3. AVG: Calculating the Average

The AVG() function calculates the average value of a numeric column.

Syntax:

sql

```
SELECT AVG(column_name)
FROM table_name
WHERE condition;
```

Example:

To find the average order amount in the Orders table:

sql

```
SELECT AVG(TotalAmount)
FROM Orders;
```

This query will return the average of the TotalAmount column across all rows in the Orders table.

4. MIN: Finding the Minimum Value

The MIN() function returns the smallest value in a specified column.

Syntax:

sql

```
SELECT MIN(column_name)
```

```
FROM table_name
WHERE condition;
```

Example:

To find the minimum order amount:

```
sql
```

```
SELECT MIN(TotalAmount)
FROM Orders;
```

This query will return the smallest value from the TotalAmount column.

5. MAX: Finding the Maximum Value

The MAX() function returns the largest value in a specified column.

Syntax:

```
sql
```

```
SELECT MAX(column_name)
FROM table_name
WHERE condition;
```

Example:

To find the largest order amount:

```sql
sql

SELECT MAX(TotalAmount)
FROM Orders;
```

This query will return the largest value in the `TotalAmount` column.

GROUP BY Clause: Grouping Data for Aggregation

The GROUP BY clause is used in SQL to group rows that have the same values in specified columns into summary rows. This is typically used with aggregate functions to perform calculations on each group of rows.

1. Syntax for GROUP BY
```sql
sql

SELECT column1, AGGREGATE_FUNCTION(column2)
FROM table_name
GROUP BY column1;
```

- AGGREGATE_FUNCTION() can be COUNT(), SUM(), AVG(), MIN(), MAX(), or any other aggregation function.
- The GROUP BY clause groups rows by column1.

109

Example:

To find the total amount spent by each customer, you can group the results by `CustomerID`:

sql

```
SELECT CustomerID, SUM(TotalAmount)
FROM Orders
GROUP BY CustomerID;
```

This query will return the total order amount for each customer, grouping the data by `CustomerID`.

2. Multiple Columns in GROUP BY

You can group by multiple columns if necessary. For instance, to find the total amount spent by each customer for each product:

sql

```
SELECT CustomerID, ProductID, SUM(TotalAmount)
FROM Orders
GROUP BY CustomerID, ProductID;
```

This will return the total amount spent by each customer for each product, grouping the data by both `CustomerID` and `ProductID`.

HAVING Clause: Filtering Results After Aggregation

The HAVING clause is used to filter records after aggregation has been performed by the GROUP BY clause. It is similar to the WHERE clause, but WHERE is used to filter rows before the aggregation, whereas HAVING filters rows after the aggregation.

1. Syntax for HAVING

sql

```
SELECT column1, AGGREGATE_FUNCTION(column2)
FROM table_name
GROUP BY column1
HAVING condition;
```

- The condition in the HAVING clause must refer to the aggregate function applied to the data.

Example:

To find customers who have spent more than $500 in total, you can use the HAVING clause:

sql

```
SELECT CustomerID, SUM(TotalAmount)
FROM Orders
GROUP BY CustomerID
HAVING SUM(TotalAmount) > 500;
```

This query will return customers who have spent more than $500 on orders.

2. Key Points about HAVING

- The HAVING clause is used to filter aggregated results.
- Unlike WHERE, which filters rows before grouping, HAVING works on aggregated data, so it must be used after GROUP BY.

Combining GROUP BY and HAVING

In practice, you often use GROUP BY with aggregate functions, and then use HAVING to filter the results of that aggregation.

Example:

To find products that have been ordered more than 10 times, you would use:

sql

```
SELECT ProductID, COUNT(OrderID) AS OrderCount
FROM OrderDetails
GROUP BY ProductID
HAVING COUNT(OrderID) > 10;
```

This query will return products that appear in more than 10 orders.

Conclusion

Aggregating data is a crucial part of SQL because it allows you to summarize large datasets in meaningful ways. Whether you're counting rows, summing totals, finding averages, or identifying the minimum or maximum values, these operations enable you to extract valuable insights from your data. By mastering functions like COUNT, SUM, AVG, MIN, and MAX, and understanding how to group and filter aggregated data using the GROUP BY and HAVING clauses, you'll be well-equipped to handle complex reporting and data analysis tasks in SQL.

CHAPTER 11

SUBQUERIES

Subqueries, also known as inner queries or nested queries, are a powerful feature of SQL that allows you to embed one query inside another. Subqueries can be used to retrieve intermediate results that are then utilized by the main query. They allow you to solve complex queries that would be difficult to express in a single query. In this chapter, we'll define subqueries, explore the different types, and examine how they can be used in SELECT, WHERE, and FROM clauses.

What is a Subquery?

A **subquery** is a query that is nested inside another SQL query. The subquery can return a single value, a list of values, or even a set of rows, depending on the context in which it is used. Subqueries are commonly used to perform operations such as filtering results based on dynamic criteria or using results from one query as input for another.

Use Cases for Subqueries:

- **Filtering results dynamically:** Subqueries allow you to filter records based on results from another query.

- **Comparing values across tables:** Subqueries are often used to compare a value in one table with values in another table.
- **Finding aggregated results:** You can use subqueries to find sums, averages, or counts that are then used in a higher-level query.

Example: Suppose you want to find customers who have made orders that are higher than the average order value. You could use a subquery to calculate the average and then compare it against each customer's order total.

sql

```
SELECT CustomerID, TotalAmount
FROM Orders
WHERE TotalAmount > (SELECT AVG(TotalAmount) FROM
Orders);
```

In this example, the subquery (SELECT AVG(TotalAmount) FROM Orders) computes the average order total, and the main query returns the customers who made orders greater than that average.

Types of Subqueries

Subqueries can be categorized into three main types based on how they are related to the outer query:

1. **Scalar Subquery**
2. **Correlated Subquery**
3. **Non-Correlated Subquery**

1. Scalar Subquery

A **scalar subquery** is a subquery that returns a single value (one row, one column). It is typically used in a WHERE, SELECT, or HAVING clause where a single value is expected.

Example:

Suppose you want to find the order with the highest TotalAmount in the Orders table:

sql

```
SELECT OrderID, TotalAmount
FROM Orders
WHERE TotalAmount = (SELECT MAX(TotalAmount) FROM
Orders);
```

Here, the scalar subquery (SELECT MAX(TotalAmount) FROM Orders) returns a single value (the highest order amount), and the main query retrieves the order that matches this value.

2. Correlated Subquery

A **correlated subquery** is a subquery that refers to a column from the outer query. This means that for each row processed by the outer query, the subquery is re-executed with values specific to that row.

Example:

Let's say you want to find customers who have made orders that are higher than the average order for their own region. A correlated subquery can help with this:

sql

```
SELECT CustomerID, TotalAmount
FROM Orders o1
WHERE TotalAmount > (SELECT AVG(TotalAmount)
                     FROM Orders o2
                     WHERE       o1.Region       =
o2.Region);
```

In this query:

- The outer query processes each Order row (o1).

117

- For each row, the correlated subquery computes the average order total for the same region (o1.Region = o2.Region).

The key difference here is that the subquery is dependent on the outer query. Each row in the outer query triggers a separate execution of the subquery.

3. Non-Correlated Subquery

A **non-correlated subquery** is a subquery that does not reference any columns from the outer query. It can be executed independently of the outer query and typically returns a single result set.

Example:

If you wanted to find all orders placed by customers whose total order amount is above the overall average, you could use a non-correlated subquery:

sql

```
SELECT CustomerID, TotalAmount
FROM Orders
WHERE TotalAmount > (SELECT AVG(TotalAmount) FROM Orders);
```

Here, the subquery is independent and does not depend on the outer query. It simply calculates the average `TotalAmount` from the entire `Orders` table and then compares each individual `TotalAmount` to that value.

Using Subqueries in SELECT, WHERE, and FROM Clauses

Subqueries can be used in several places within a SQL query, including the `SELECT`, `WHERE`, and `FROM` clauses.

1. Subqueries in the SELECT Clause

Subqueries in the `SELECT` clause can be used to compute values dynamically for each row in the result set.

Example:

If you want to list each customer's total order amount and the highest order amount from the same customer, you could use a subquery in the `SELECT` clause:

sql

```
SELECT CustomerID,
       TotalAmount,
       (SELECT   MAX(TotalAmount)   FROM   Orders
WHERE    CustomerID    =    o.CustomerID)    AS
MaxOrderAmount
```

```
FROM Orders o;
```

This query will return each order's `TotalAmount` along with the highest `TotalAmount` for the corresponding customer.

2. Subqueries in the WHERE Clause

Subqueries in the `WHERE` clause are commonly used for filtering results based on the result of another query. This is the most common use of subqueries.

Example:

If you want to find customers who have placed orders that are above the average order amount:

```sql
sql

SELECT CustomerID, TotalAmount
FROM Orders
WHERE TotalAmount > (SELECT AVG(TotalAmount) FROM
Orders);
```

This query filters the orders to only include those whose `TotalAmount` is greater than the overall average.

3. Subqueries in the FROM Clause

Subqueries in the FROM clause are sometimes called **inline views**. These subqueries are treated as temporary tables for the duration of the query execution.

Example:

You might use a subquery in the FROM clause to calculate aggregated data before performing additional operations:

sql

```
SELECT    CustomerID,    SUM(TotalAmount)    AS
TotalSpent
FROM (SELECT CustomerID, TotalAmount FROM Orders
WHERE OrderDate > '2022-01-01') AS RecentOrders
GROUP BY CustomerID;
```

Here, the subquery (SELECT CustomerID, TotalAmount FROM Orders WHERE OrderDate > '2022-01-01') **acts as a temporary table, filtering the orders placed after January 1, 2022. The outer query then groups the results and sums the** TotalAmount **for each customer.**

Conclusion

Subqueries are an essential tool in SQL, enabling you to solve complex queries by nesting one query inside another. They can be used in different ways to return values, compare rows, and perform calculations. Understanding the different types of subqueries—scalar, correlated, and non-correlated—and knowing how to use them in SELECT, WHERE, and FROM clauses, will greatly enhance your ability to manipulate and query data effectively. Whether you are filtering results, comparing values, or calculating aggregates, subqueries provide a flexible and powerful way to enhance your SQL queries.

CHAPTER 12

MODIFYING DATA

In SQL, data modification is a key operation that allows you to manipulate the records stored in your tables. This chapter will explore the three main SQL statements used for modifying data: UPDATE, DELETE, and INSERT. We will delve into the syntax, practical examples, and the differences between these statements so you can confidently apply them to your database.

UPDATE Statement: Changing Existing Data in Your Tables

The UPDATE statement in SQL allows you to modify the values of one or more columns in an existing row or rows in a table. It's a powerful tool when you need to update specific data without altering the entire table.

Syntax:

```sql

UPDATE table_name
SET column1 = value1, column2 = value2, ...
WHERE condition;
```

123

- `table_name`: The name of the table where the data will be updated.
- `column1, column2`: The columns that you want to update.
- `value1, value2`: The new values that you want to assign to the respective columns.
- `WHERE condition`: The condition that specifies which rows to update. Without this condition, all rows in the table will be updated.

Example:

If you want to update the email address of a customer in the `Customers` table:

```
sql

UPDATE Customers
SET Email = 'newemail@example.com'
WHERE CustomerID = 101;
```

This query will change the email address for the customer with `CustomerID` 101 to `newemail@example.com`.

Important Notes:

- Always use the `WHERE` clause to specify the rows that need to be updated. Without it, the `UPDATE` statement will apply to all rows in the table, potentially leading to unintended changes.

- If you want to update multiple columns at once, you can do so by separating each column-value pair with commas.

Example:

Updating both the email and phone number for a customer:

sql

```
UPDATE Customers
SET Email = 'newemail@example.com', Phone = '123-456-7890'
WHERE CustomerID = 101;
```

This will update both the email and phone number for the customer with CustomerID 101.

DELETE Statement: Safely Deleting Rows

The DELETE statement is used to remove one or more rows from a table. It's a permanent operation, so caution is needed when using it, especially when deleting large amounts of data.

Syntax:

sql

```
DELETE FROM table_name
WHERE condition;
```

- `table_name`: The name of the table from which you want to delete rows.
- `WHERE condition`: The condition that identifies which rows to delete. If you omit this clause, all rows in the table will be deleted, which is a dangerous operation.

Example:

If you want to delete a customer from the `Customers` table:

sql

```
DELETE FROM Customers
WHERE CustomerID = 101;
```

This query will delete the customer with `CustomerID` 101 from the `Customers` table.

Important Notes:

- Always use the `WHERE` clause to limit the rows that are deleted. Omitting the `WHERE` clause will delete all records from the table.
- Deleting rows from a table can affect related data, especially if foreign keys are in place. Ensure you handle

126

referential integrity before performing deletion operations.

Example:

To delete multiple customers who haven't placed any orders:

sql

```
DELETE FROM Customers
WHERE CustomerID NOT IN (SELECT CustomerID FROM
Orders);
```

This query will delete customers who do not have any corresponding records in the Orders table.

INSERT vs UPDATE vs DELETE: When to Use Each

While the INSERT, UPDATE, and DELETE statements all modify data in a table, they are used for different purposes and scenarios. Here's a breakdown of when to use each statement:

1. INSERT:

The INSERT statement is used when you want to add new records to a table.

127

- **Use it when:** You are adding new rows of data to the table.
- **Example:** Adding a new customer to the Customers table.

sql

```
INSERT INTO Customers (CustomerID, Name, Email)
VALUES (102, 'John Doe', 'johndoe@example.com');
```

- **Note:** The INSERT statement can also be used to insert multiple rows at once by separating each set of values with commas.

2. UPDATE:

The UPDATE statement is used to modify existing data within a table.

- **Use it when:** You need to update one or more columns of existing records in a table.
- **Example:** Changing the email address of an existing customer.

sql

```
UPDATE Customers
SET Email = 'newemail@example.com'
WHERE CustomerID = 102;
```

- **Note:** Be careful with the WHERE clause to ensure that only the intended records are updated.

3. DELETE:

The DELETE statement is used to remove one or more records from a table.

- **Use it when:** You need to remove rows that are no longer needed or are irrelevant.
- **Example:** Deleting a customer who no longer wants to remain in the database.

sql

```
DELETE FROM Customers
WHERE CustomerID = 102;
```

- **Note:** Always make sure to use the WHERE clause when deleting records to avoid deleting all rows in the table.

Conclusion

Understanding when and how to use the UPDATE, DELETE, and INSERT statements is essential for efficiently managing your database.

- **INSERT** is used to add new records.

- **UPDATE** is used to modify existing data.

- **DELETE** is used to remove records that are no longer needed.

Each statement has its place in maintaining a clean, accurate, and up-to-date database. Always use caution, particularly with UPDATE and DELETE, as these statements can make permanent changes to your data. Use the WHERE clause to limit the scope of these changes and avoid accidentally modifying or deleting more data than intended.

CHAPTER 13

DATABASE CONSTRAINTS

Database constraints are rules that help maintain the integrity and accuracy of data in a relational database. They ensure that the data stored in the database adheres to specific requirements, reducing the likelihood of errors and ensuring consistency across related tables. In this chapter, we will explore the different types of database constraints, including primary keys, foreign keys, unique, not null, default, and check constraints. By the end of this chapter, you'll understand how to apply constraints to your tables to ensure data integrity.

Primary Keys and Foreign Keys: Defining Relationships Between Tables

1. Primary Key

A **primary key** is a unique identifier for each record in a table. It ensures that each row can be uniquely identified by a combination of columns, usually a single column. The primary key constraint guarantees that no two rows in a table have the same primary key value. A primary key also cannot contain NULL values.

- **Purpose:** The primary key is used to uniquely identify records in a table and is often the main way of referencing records in relationships with other tables.
- **Key Characteristics:**
  - Uniqueness: Every value in the primary key column(s) must be unique.
  - Not NULL: Primary key columns cannot contain NULL values.
  - One primary key per table: Each table can only have one primary key.

Example:

If you are creating a `Customers` table, you might use `CustomerID` as the primary key.

sql

```sql
CREATE TABLE Customers (
    CustomerID INT PRIMARY KEY,
    Name VARCHAR(100),
    Email VARCHAR(100)
);
```

In this example, `CustomerID` is the primary key for the `Customers` table. Each customer must have a unique `CustomerID` that can be used to identify them.

2. Foreign Key

A **foreign key** is a column (or set of columns) in one table that is used to link to the primary key of another table. This defines a relationship between the two tables and enforces referential integrity by ensuring that the values in the foreign key column(s) exist in the referenced table.

- **Purpose:** Foreign keys help maintain data integrity across related tables by ensuring that relationships between records are valid.
- **Key Characteristics:**
    o The foreign key column(s) must match the primary key of the referenced table or must be NULL.
    o Foreign keys can establish one-to-many or many-to-many relationships.

Example:

If you have an Orders table, you can define a foreign key that links each order to a specific customer:

sql

```
CREATE TABLE Orders (
    OrderID INT PRIMARY KEY,
    OrderDate DATE,
```

133

```
CustomerID INT,
    FOREIGN    KEY    (CustomerID)    REFERENCES
Customers(CustomerID)
);
```

Here, `CustomerID` in the `Orders` table is a foreign key that references the `CustomerID` in the `Customers` table. This means that every order must belong to an existing customer. If you try to insert an order with a non-existent `CustomerID`, the database will reject the operation.

Unique, Not Null, and Default Constraints: Ensuring Data Integrity

1. Unique Constraint

The **unique constraint** ensures that all values in a column (or a combination of columns) are unique across all rows in the table. This is similar to the primary key, but unlike the primary key, a column with a unique constraint can allow NULL values.

- **Purpose:** The unique constraint helps ensure that there are no duplicate values in the specified column(s), which is important for maintaining the accuracy of data.
- **Key Characteristics:**
  - Unique: Ensures that all values are distinct.

134

o NULL values are allowed: Unlike primary keys, unique constraints can allow NULLs, but only one NULL per column.

Example:

If you want to ensure that email addresses in the `Customers` table are unique:

sql

```
CREATE TABLE Customers (
    CustomerID INT PRIMARY KEY,
    Name VARCHAR(100),
    Email VARCHAR(100) UNIQUE
);
```

This ensures that no two customers can have the same email address.

2. Not Null Constraint

The **not null constraint** ensures that a column cannot contain NULL values. This is used when a field must always have a value, ensuring that no incomplete or missing data is stored.

- **Purpose:** The not null constraint is used to ensure that important data is not left empty.
- **Key Characteristics:**

135

o Prevents NULL values: It forces the column to always contain a valid value.

Example:

If you want to make sure that every customer has a `Name` and `Email`, you can define those columns as NOT NULL:

sql

```
CREATE TABLE Customers (
    CustomerID INT PRIMARY KEY,
    Name VARCHAR(100) NOT NULL,
    Email VARCHAR(100) NOT NULL
);
```

Here, both `Name` and `Email` columns must contain a value when a new row is inserted into the `Customers` table.

3. Default Constraint

The **default constraint** provides a default value for a column when no value is specified during an INSERT operation. This is helpful when you want to ensure that certain columns always have a value, even if the user doesn't provide one.

- **Purpose:** The default constraint automatically fills a column with a default value if no value is provided during an insert.

136

- **Key Characteristics:**
  - Automatically assigns a value: If a value for the column is not specified during insertion, the default value is applied.
  - Can be used for both strings and numbers, or even complex expressions.

Example:

If you want to automatically set the `Status` column of the `Orders` table to `'Pending'` when a new order is inserted:

sql

```
CREATE TABLE Orders (
    OrderID INT PRIMARY KEY,
    OrderDate DATE,
    Status VARCHAR(50) DEFAULT 'Pending'
);
```

Here, if no status is provided during the insertion of a new order, the `Status` column will default to `'Pending'`.

Check Constraints: Enforcing Business Rules at the Database Level

The **check constraint** ensures that the values in a column meet a specific condition or business rule. It's used to enforce rules such as range constraints, value restrictions, or any condition that data must satisfy.

- **Purpose:** The check constraint allows you to define a condition that must be true for every row in the table.
- **Key Characteristics:**
    - The condition can be any valid SQL expression (e.g., comparisons, logical operators).
    - It is applied when inserting or updating data.

Example:

If you want to ensure that the Age column in the Employees table contains only valid ages (greater than 18), you can use a check constraint:

sql

```
CREATE TABLE Employees (
    EmployeeID INT PRIMARY KEY,
    Name VARCHAR(100),
    Age INT CHECK (Age > 18)
);
```

In this example, the Age must be greater than 18. Any attempt to insert or update a record with an Age value less than or equal to 18 will result in an error.

Conclusion

Database constraints are essential for maintaining data integrity and ensuring that your database operates according to the defined rules. By using primary keys, foreign keys, unique, not null, default, and check constraints, you can:

- **Maintain relationships** between tables and prevent inconsistent data.
- **Ensure data integrity** by avoiding duplicate or missing values.
- **Enforce business rules** directly at the database level, preventing invalid data from being inserted.

These constraints help you design more robust, reliable, and consistent databases, ensuring that your data remains accurate and trustworthy throughout its lifecycle.

CHAPTER 14

INDEXING FOR PERFORMANCE

Indexes are a fundamental tool for improving the performance of queries in a relational database. By providing a faster way to look up data, indexes can drastically speed up the retrieval of records. However, while indexes can be incredibly useful for optimizing read-heavy operations, they also come with trade-offs. In this chapter, we will explore the concept of indexing, when and why to use indexes, and the potential limitations and pitfalls of indexing.

What Are Indexes? How They Speed Up Queries

An **index** is a data structure that improves the speed of data retrieval operations on a database table. It is similar to an index in a book — it allows the database to find specific rows of data quickly without having to search through the entire table.

How Indexes Work:

When you create an index on one or more columns of a table, the database builds a separate structure that organizes the values of those columns in a way that makes it easier and faster to look them up. The most common type of index is a **B-tree index**, but there are other types such as hash indexes, full-text indexes, and spatial indexes, depending on the database system.

- **B-tree Indexes:** These are the most commonly used index type, where the database organizes data in a balanced tree structure, allowing for efficient lookups, insertions, and deletions.
- **Hash Indexes:** Used for equality comparisons, hash indexes store data in a way that allows quick access based on a hash value.
- **Full-text Indexes:** Useful for indexing large text fields, such as articles or descriptions, enabling fast text searching.
- **Spatial Indexes:** Used to store and query spatial data, such as geographic coordinates.

Example:

Imagine you have a `Customers` table with thousands of rows. If you frequently query customers by their last name, you could create an index on the `LastName` column. This index would allow the database to locate matching customers much faster than if it had to scan the entire table.

sql

```sql
CREATE INDEX idx_lastname ON Customers (LastName);
```

Now, queries like the following would be much faster:

```sql
SELECT * FROM Customers WHERE LastName = 'Smith';
```

Instead of scanning the entire `Customers` table for rows with `LastName = 'Smith'`, the database can quickly look up the index and retrieve the matching rows.

When to Use Indexes: Optimizing SELECT Queries

Indexes are most beneficial when you perform queries that search, sort, or join large tables. They are primarily used to optimize **SELECT** queries, especially those with `WHERE`, `JOIN`, or `ORDER BY` clauses.

1. Optimizing Searches (WHERE Clause)

Indexes can significantly speed up searches, especially when searching for specific values in a large dataset. By indexing columns that are frequently used in the `WHERE` clause, the database can quickly locate matching rows.

Example:

If you often query the `Customers` table based on the `Email` column:

sql

```
SELECT * FROM Customers WHERE Email = 'customer@example.com';
```

Creating an index on the `Email` column will speed up this query:

sql

```
CREATE INDEX idx_email ON Customers (Email);
```

2. Optimizing Sorting (ORDER BY Clause)

Indexes can also speed up queries that sort results using the `ORDER BY` clause. When you query a table and request the results to be sorted by a specific column, an index on that column can reduce the need for a full table scan and sorting at query time.

Example:

If you frequently query customer data sorted by their `LastName`, an index on `LastName` will help speed up these queries:

sql

```
SELECT * FROM Customers ORDER BY LastName;
```

3. Optimizing Joins (JOIN Clause)

When performing JOIN operations, indexes on the columns that are used in the join condition (often foreign keys and primary keys) can drastically improve performance. The database can use the index to quickly locate matching rows in the related table.

Example:

Consider a query that joins Orders and Customers on the CustomerID:

sql

```
SELECT o.OrderID, c.Name
FROM Orders o
JOIN Customers c ON o.CustomerID = c.CustomerID;
```

Creating an index on CustomerID in both the Orders and Customers tables will improve the performance of this query:

sql

```
CREATE INDEX idx_customer_id ON Orders
(CustomerID);
CREATE INDEX idx_customer_id_customers ON
Customers (CustomerID);
```

Limitations and Pitfalls of Indexing

While indexes can significantly speed up query performance, they are not without their drawbacks. Understanding these limitations is crucial for using indexes effectively.

1. Performance Trade-offs for Write Operations

Indexes are primarily designed to improve **read performance** (i.e., for SELECT queries). However, they come with a cost. When you insert, update, or delete records, the database must also update the index to reflect the changes in the underlying data. This can slow down write operations, especially when there are many indexes on a table.

Example:

Inserting a new record into a table with multiple indexes means that the database must update each index with the new record's values. This can slow down the insertion process, particularly in large tables with numerous indexes.

2. Increased Storage Requirements

Indexes require additional disk space. The more indexes you create, the more storage your database will need. While individual indexes don't usually take up a lot of space, if you index multiple columns or create a large number of indexes, this can add up.

Example:

In the case of very large databases, indexing every column can lead to excessive storage use, which may affect performance, especially in systems with limited storage capacity.

3. Maintenance Overhead

Indexes need to be maintained as data changes. When rows are inserted, updated, or deleted, the index structure may need to be reorganized to maintain its efficiency. This can result in extra CPU and disk I/O operations.

For instance, in a heavily updated table, an index may become fragmented over time, meaning that the database has to spend additional resources to keep the index optimized. Regular **index rebuilding** or **reorganization** can help mitigate this, but it introduces additional maintenance tasks.

4. Over-Indexing Can Be Harmful

Creating too many indexes can actually degrade performance, particularly when it comes to write-heavy workloads. Each additional index adds overhead to data manipulation operations (INSERT, UPDATE, DELETE), so it's essential to strike a balance between indexing and maintaining good write performance.

146

Example:

If you create an index on every column of a large table, the database will have to update each index whenever data is modified, leading to performance degradation during write operations.

Conclusion

Indexes are a powerful tool for optimizing query performance in SQL databases, particularly when dealing with large datasets and complex queries. By using indexes effectively, you can speed up data retrieval and enhance overall query performance, especially for SELECT queries, sorting, and joins.

However, it's important to carefully consider when and where to apply indexes. Indexes are not a one-size-fits-all solution; they can introduce overhead during write operations, require additional storage space, and need regular maintenance. A thoughtful approach to indexing, based on the specific needs of your queries and data usage patterns, will ensure that your database performs optimally without overburdening resources.

CHAPTER 15

NORMALIZATION

Database normalization is a fundamental concept in database design aimed at organizing data efficiently to reduce redundancy and improve data integrity. By following normalization principles, you ensure that your database is logically structured, reduces the chances of data anomalies, and supports efficient data manipulation. However, normalization does come with trade-offs, and sometimes denormalization may be necessary for performance reasons. In this chapter, we will explore the importance of database normalization, the different normal forms (1st, 2nd, and 3rd), and discuss when denormalization might be beneficial.

What is Database Normalization? Why It's Important for Efficient Design

Database normalization is the process of organizing the attributes and relationships of a database to minimize redundancy and dependency. The goal is to structure data so that it's logically stored, making it easier to manage, retrieve, and update.

Key Benefits of Normalization:

1. **Minimized Data Redundancy:** By splitting data into smaller, related tables, normalization reduces the chances of repeating information across multiple rows.

2. **Improved Data Integrity:** It ensures that the data is consistent, eliminating issues such as contradictory or outdated information.

3. **Easier Maintenance:** Well-structured databases are easier to maintain, update, and extend over time.

Without normalization, databases can quickly become difficult to manage and prone to errors. For instance, if you store customer information, including multiple addresses, in a single table, any changes to a customer's address may require multiple updates in the same table. This increases the risk of data inconsistency and anomalies.

The 1st, 2nd, and 3rd Normal Forms: Step-by-Step Breakdown

Normalization is done in steps, with each step known as a **normal form** (NF). The process involves ensuring that a database schema adheres to specific rules, reducing redundancy and ensuring consistency at each level. There are several normal forms, but the most commonly used are the **1st Normal Form (1NF), 2nd**

Normal Form (2NF), and **3rd Normal Form (3NF)**. Let's break each one down.

1st Normal Form (1NF): Eliminate Duplicate Columns and Ensure Atomicity

A table is in **1st Normal Form (1NF)** if it satisfies the following conditions:

- **Atomicity:** All columns must contain atomic (indivisible) values. This means that each column should store only one value per row, not a set or list of values.
- **Uniqueness:** Each row in the table must be unique, meaning there must be a primary key that uniquely identifies each record.
- **No Repeating Groups:** A table should not contain multiple columns that represent the same type of data (i.e., no columns like `Phone1`, `Phone2`, `Phone3`).

Example:

Consider a table storing customer information with multiple phone numbers:

CustomerID	Name	Phone Numbers
1	John Doe	555-1234, 555-5678

CustomerID	Name	Phone Numbers
2	Jane Smith	555-8765

This table is not in 1NF because the `Phone Numbers` column contains multiple values. To convert this table into 1NF, we would separate the phone numbers into distinct rows:

CustomerID	Name	Phone Number
1	John Doe	555-1234
1	John Doe	555-5678
2	Jane Smith	555-8765

Now, each column contains atomic values, and the table is in 1NF.

2nd Normal Form (2NF): Eliminate Partial Dependencies

A table is in **2nd Normal Form (2NF)** if it is in **1NF** and all non-key attributes are fully functionally dependent on the entire primary key. This rule is important when dealing with composite primary keys (primary keys made up of more than one column).

- **No Partial Dependencies:** Any non-key attribute must depend on the whole primary key, not just part of it.

151

Example:

Consider a table storing order details with a composite primary key consisting of OrderID and ProductID:

OrderID	ProductID	ProductName	Quantity
1	101	Widget	5
1	102	Gadget	3
2	101	Widget	7

In this example, ProductName depends only on ProductID, not on the entire primary key (OrderID and ProductID). This creates a **partial dependency**.

To bring the table into 2NF, we would split the table into two:

1. **Orders Table:**

OrderID	ProductID	Quantity
1	101	5
1	102	3
2	101	7

2. **Products Table:**

ProductID	ProductName
101	Widget
102	Gadget

Now, the `ProductName` attribute is dependent on the entire `ProductID`, not just part of the primary key. The data is now in 2NF.

3rd Normal Form (3NF): Eliminate Transitive Dependencies

A table is in **3rd Normal Form (3NF)** if it is in **2NF** and all non-key attributes are not transitively dependent on the primary key.

- **No Transitive Dependencies:** Non-key attributes should not depend on other non-key attributes. In simpler terms, each non-key column should depend directly on the primary key and not on another non-key column.

Example:

Consider a table where `Employee` details are stored along with the department the employee belongs to:

EmployeeID	EmployeeName	DepartmentID	DepartmentName
1	John Smith	10	Sales
2	Jane Doe	20	Marketing

In this case, DepartmentName is dependent on DepartmentID, not on EmployeeID. This is a **transitive dependency**, meaning that DepartmentName indirectly depends on the EmployeeID through the DepartmentID.

To bring the table into 3NF, we would split the data into two tables:

1. **Employees Table:**

EmployeeID	EmployeeName	DepartmentID
1	John Smith	10
2	Jane Doe	20

2. **Departments Table:**

154

DepartmentID	DepartmentName
10	Sales
20	Marketing

Now, there are no transitive dependencies, and the table is in 3NF.

Dealing with Denormalization: When to Go Against Normalization

While normalization helps create efficient and maintainable databases, it can sometimes result in performance issues, especially when dealing with large datasets and complex queries. Denormalization is the process of introducing redundancy into a database by combining tables that were previously split through normalization.

When to Denormalize:

Denormalization may be considered in the following scenarios:

1. **Performance Optimization:** In cases where performance is critical, such as for reporting or analytics applications, denormalization can help reduce the number of joins and speed up read operations.
2. **Complex Queries:** For complex queries that require many joins, denormalization can reduce the

155

computational cost by consolidating data into fewer tables.

3. **Read-Heavy Workloads:** If the application has a predominantly read-heavy workload (e.g., online reporting), denormalizing certain parts of the database can improve query performance.

Example of Denormalization:

If a reporting system frequently requires data from multiple tables and joins are too costly, you might denormalize the Orders and Customers tables by merging them into a single table. While this increases redundancy (e.g., customer details stored with every order), it can speed up read queries that need to display customer order details.

sql

```
CREATE TABLE DenormalizedOrders (
    OrderID INT PRIMARY KEY,
    OrderDate DATE,
    CustomerID INT,
    CustomerName VARCHAR(100),
    CustomerEmail VARCHAR(100),
    OrderAmount DECIMAL
);
```

In this case, `CustomerName` and `CustomerEmail` are duplicated for each order, but the trade-off is faster query performance for certain use cases.

Conclusion

Normalization is a key concept in database design, promoting data integrity, reducing redundancy, and ensuring logical relationships between data elements. By adhering to **1st**, **2nd**, and **3rd Normal Forms**, you can create a well-structured database that is easier to manage and maintain. However, as with most things in technology, there's no one-size-fits-all solution. In some cases, **denormalization** may be necessary to optimize performance, especially in read-heavy applications. Understanding when and why to normalize or denormalize data will allow you to strike the right balance between data integrity and system performance.

CHAPTER 16

SQL TRANSACTIONS

In real-world database systems, operations often involve multiple steps that must either all succeed or all fail together. A single operation in a database might consist of several individual tasks: inserting records, updating values, or deleting data. SQL transactions are a powerful mechanism that allows you to group these multiple tasks into one logical unit of work. By using transactions, you can ensure that your database remains in a consistent state, even if errors occur during execution.

In this chapter, we will explore **SQL transactions**, understand their significance, and discuss the **ACID properties** that guarantee data integrity. Additionally, we will cover how to manage transactions using commands like **COMMIT**, **ROLLBACK**, and **SAVEPOINT** to control transaction flow effectively.

What is a Transaction?

A **transaction** in SQL is a sequence of one or more SQL operations that are executed as a single unit. Transactions ensure that the database changes only if all operations in the sequence succeed. If any part of the transaction fails, the entire transaction is rolled back to maintain the integrity of the database.

Think of a transaction like a batch of instructions. For example, imagine transferring money from one bank account to another. This operation involves two steps:

1. Deducting the amount from the sender's account.
2. Adding the same amount to the recipient's account.

If one step fails (e.g., due to insufficient funds), we don't want the deduction to happen without the addition to the recipient's account, as this would create an inconsistent state. Transactions ensure that either both steps succeed, or neither does.

ACID Properties: Ensuring Data Integrity with Transactions

Transactions are governed by the **ACID** properties, which are the core principles ensuring data integrity and reliability in a database system. These properties stand for:

1. **Atomicity:**
   - **Definition:** Atomicity ensures that all operations within a transaction are treated as a single unit. The transaction is either fully completed (committed) or not executed at all (rolled back).

- o **Example:** In a banking system, if a money transfer transaction includes multiple updates (e.g., debiting one account and crediting another), atomicity guarantees that either both operations will succeed or both will fail, leaving no half-completed actions.

2. **Consistency:**
   - o **Definition:** A transaction brings the database from one valid state to another. The database must always be in a valid state before and after the transaction.
   - o **Example:** If a transaction involves transferring funds from one account to another, the total amount of money in both accounts must remain consistent before and after the transaction.

3. **Isolation:**
   - o **Definition:** Isolation ensures that transactions are executed independently of one another, even when they are running concurrently. Changes made by one transaction are not visible to other transactions until the transaction is committed.
   - o **Example:** If two transactions are trying to transfer money from the same account at the same time, isolation ensures that one transaction completes before the other begins, preventing issues like overdrafts or double-spending.

4. **Durability:**

   o **Definition:** Once a transaction has been committed, its changes are permanent, even if the system crashes. The database guarantees that committed data will not be lost.

   o **Example:** After transferring money, even if the system crashes immediately after the commit, the money transfer is permanent, and the records will not be lost.

Together, these properties ensure that SQL transactions provide reliable and predictable behavior, which is essential for maintaining the integrity of a database, especially in critical systems like finance and healthcare.

COMMIT, ROLLBACK, and SAVEPOINT: Managing Transaction Flow

Managing transactions is crucial for controlling how data is modified within a database. SQL provides several commands to manage the flow of a transaction:

COMMIT: Making Changes Permanent

The **COMMIT** statement is used to save the changes made during a transaction to the database. Once a transaction is committed, all changes are permanent and cannot be undone unless explicitly rolled back by a future transaction.

Example of COMMIT:

```sql

BEGIN TRANSACTION;

UPDATE Accounts
SET Balance = Balance - 100
WHERE AccountID = 1;

UPDATE Accounts
SET Balance = Balance + 100
WHERE AccountID = 2;

COMMIT;
```

In this example, after the updates to the `Accounts` table are completed, the **COMMIT** statement ensures that the changes are saved to the database. If there is no COMMIT, the transaction will not be finalized.

ROLLBACK: Undoing Changes

The **ROLLBACK** statement is used to undo all changes made during the transaction, returning the database to the state it was in before the transaction began. This is especially useful if an error occurs and you want to revert the changes.

Example of ROLLBACK:

sql

```
BEGIN TRANSACTION;

UPDATE Accounts
SET Balance = Balance - 100
WHERE AccountID = 1;

UPDATE Accounts
SET Balance = Balance + 100
WHERE AccountID = 2;

-- Oops! Something went wrong, so we rollback the
transaction
ROLLBACK;
```

In this case, if an error occurs after the first update (e.g., if the second update fails), the **ROLLBACK** statement ensures that none of the changes are committed to the database. The data is restored to its original state before the transaction began.

SAVEPOINT: Creating Intermediate Checkpoints

A **SAVEPOINT** allows you to create a named point within a transaction. You can then **ROLLBACK** to a savepoint, undoing part of the transaction while keeping earlier changes intact. This is useful when you want to perform some complex operations but still have the option to roll back to a safe point in case of failure.

Example of SAVEPOINT:

```sql

BEGIN TRANSACTION;

UPDATE Accounts
SET Balance = Balance - 100
WHERE AccountID = 1;

SAVEPOINT BeforeTransfer;

UPDATE Accounts
SET Balance = Balance + 100
WHERE AccountID = 2;

-- Something goes wrong here, so we roll back to
BeforeTransfer
ROLLBACK TO SAVEPOINT BeforeTransfer;

COMMIT;
```

In this example, the changes made before the SAVEPOINT BeforeTransfer are preserved, but any changes made after that point (e.g., the second update to AccountID = 2) are undone. The **COMMIT** at the end ensures that the transaction is finalized, but only the successful changes will be saved.

Best Practices for Using Transactions

1. **Keep Transactions Short:** Long-running transactions can lock database resources, preventing other operations from executing. Try to keep transactions as short as possible by executing only necessary commands within the transaction.

2. **Handle Errors Gracefully:** Always use TRY...CATCH blocks (in SQL systems that support them) to handle exceptions and ensure that **ROLLBACK** is executed in case of errors.

3. **Use SAVEPOINT for Complex Transactions:** When dealing with multiple steps in a transaction, use **SAVEPOINT** to create intermediate checkpoints. This provides more control over what parts of a transaction are rolled back.

4. **Avoid Overuse of Transactions:** While transactions are essential for data consistency, overusing them or keeping them open for too long can lead to performance bottlenecks. Ensure transactions are used strategically.

Conclusion

SQL transactions are a powerful mechanism that ensures the reliability and consistency of your database. By following the **ACID** properties—**Atomicity**, **Consistency**, **Isolation**, and **Durability**—you can maintain data integrity and prevent anomalies. Commands like **COMMIT**, **ROLLBACK**, and **SAVEPOINT** give you control over transaction flow, allowing you to commit changes, undo operations, and create safe points within a transaction. Mastering transactions is essential for managing complex data operations and ensuring that your database remains in a reliable state, even in the face of errors or system crashes.

CHAPTER 17

ADVANCED QUERYING TECHNIQUES

Once you're comfortable with basic SQL queries, it's time to dive into more advanced techniques that can take your querying skills to the next level. In this chapter, we'll explore how to introduce **conditional logic**, handle **NULL values** more effectively, and leverage **window functions** for advanced data analysis. These advanced querying techniques will empower you to write more powerful and flexible SQL queries, and help you solve complex data challenges.

CASE Statements: Implementing Conditional Logic in SQL

The **CASE** statement in SQL is like an "if-else" or "switch" statement in traditional programming languages. It allows you to implement conditional logic directly in your queries. This is particularly useful when you need to change the result based on certain conditions without having to modify the underlying data.

Syntax:

sql

```
SELECT column_name,
       CASE
            WHEN condition THEN result
            WHEN condition THEN result
            ELSE result
       END AS alias_name
FROM table_name;
```

Example:

Suppose you want to categorize employees based on their salary into different salary ranges. Instead of creating multiple queries or modifying the database, you can use a CASE statement:

sql

```
SELECT employee_name,
       salary,
       CASE
            WHEN salary > 100000 THEN 'High'
            WHEN salary BETWEEN 50000 AND 100000
THEN 'Medium'
            ELSE 'Low'
       END AS salary_category
FROM employees;
```

In this example:

- Employees earning more than 100,000 are labeled as "High".

168

- Employees earning between 50,000 and 100,000 are labeled as "Medium".
- All others are labeled as "Low".

The **CASE** statement allows you to categorize data or conditionally transform results within the query, making it an essential tool for data analysis and reporting.

Using COALESCE and NULLIF: Handling NULLs in Queries

SQL queries often involve dealing with **NULL values**, which represent missing or unknown data. There are specific functions designed to handle NULLs, helping to make your queries more robust and return cleaner results. Two of the most common functions for handling NULL values are **COALESCE** and **NULLIF**.

COALESCE:

The **COALESCE** function returns the first non-NULL value in a list of arguments. This is useful for replacing NULL values with a default value.

Syntax:

sql

```
COALESCE(value1, value2, ..., valueN);
```

169

Example:

Imagine you have a column for a user's middle name, but some users don't have one, so their middle name is NULL. You can use COALESCE to display "N/A" in place of NULL values.

sql

```
SELECT first_name,
       COALESCE(middle_name,       'N/A')       AS
middle_name,
       last_name
FROM users;
```

In this query:

- If middle_name is NULL, the query will return "N/A" instead.

NULLIF:

The **NULLIF** function compares two expressions and returns **NULL** if the two expressions are equal. Otherwise, it returns the first expression. This can be useful when you want to avoid returning certain values (e.g., avoid division by zero errors).

Syntax:

sql

```
NULLIF(expression1, expression2);
```

Example:

Let's say you want to divide two columns, but one of the columns may contain zero, which would cause a division by zero error. You can use **NULLIF** to handle this:

sql

```
SELECT amount,
       price,
       amount / NULLIF(price, 0) AS total_cost
FROM products;
```

In this example, if `price` is zero, **NULLIF** will return NULL, preventing a division by zero error and ensuring the query runs smoothly.

Window Functions: ROW_NUMBER, RANK, and More for Advanced Result Sets

Window functions are a powerful feature in SQL that allow you to perform calculations across a set of table rows that are somehow related to the current row, all without collapsing the result set. Unlike aggregation functions, window functions do not group rows into a single output row. Instead, they provide a value for each row based on its position relative to other rows.

ROW_NUMBER:

The **ROW_NUMBER** function assigns a unique sequential integer to rows within a partition of the result set, based on the order defined in the query.

Syntax:
sql

```
ROW_NUMBER() OVER (PARTITION BY partition_column
ORDER BY order_column);
```

Example:

Suppose you have a list of employees, and you want to rank them by their salary within each department:

sql

```
SELECT employee_name,
       department,
       salary,
       ROW_NUMBER()     OVER     (PARTITION     BY
department ORDER BY salary DESC) AS rank
FROM employees;
```

In this example:

- **ROW_NUMBER** assigns a rank to each employee within their department, ordered by salary in descending order.

RANK and DENSE_RANK:

Both **RANK** and **DENSE_RANK** are similar to **ROW_NUMBER**, but they behave differently when there are ties (rows with the same values).

- **RANK** assigns the same rank to tied rows but skips the subsequent ranks.
- **DENSE_RANK** also assigns the same rank to tied rows but does not skip the subsequent ranks.

Syntax:
sql

```
RANK() OVER (PARTITION BY partition_column ORDER
BY order_column);
DENSE_RANK() OVER (PARTITION BY partition_column
ORDER BY order_column);
```

Example of RANK:
sql

```
SELECT employee_name,
       salary,
       RANK() OVER (ORDER BY salary DESC) AS rank
```

173

```
FROM employees;
```

Here:

- Employees with the same salary will receive the same rank, but the next rank will be skipped. For example, if two employees are ranked 1, the next rank will be 3.

Example of DENSE_RANK:
sql

```
SELECT employee_name,
       salary,
       DENSE_RANK() OVER (ORDER BY salary DESC)
AS rank
FROM employees;
```

Here:

- Employees with the same salary will receive the same rank, but the next rank will be 2, not 3.

Other Window Functions:

There are several other window functions you can use to perform more advanced calculations. Some common ones include:

- **NTILE(n):** Divides rows into n roughly equal parts.

- **LEAD and LAG:** Access data from the next or previous row in the result set, respectively.

For example, if you wanted to compare an employee's salary to their next highest salary in the same department, you could use the **LEAD** function:

```sql
SELECT employee_name,
       department,
       salary,
       LEAD(salary)    OVER    (PARTITION    BY
department ORDER BY salary DESC) AS next_salary
FROM employees;
```

Conclusion

In this chapter, we explored several advanced querying techniques in SQL that can greatly enhance the flexibility and power of your queries. The **CASE** statement allows you to introduce conditional logic directly into your queries, while **COALESCE** and **NULLIF** help you handle NULL values more effectively. **Window functions** like **ROW_NUMBER**, **RANK**, and **DENSE_RANK** enable advanced data analysis by allowing you to rank, partition, and compare data in new ways, all without collapsing the result set.

Mastering these advanced techniques will help you handle more complex querying scenarios and provide greater insights into your data. Whether you're working on reporting, analytics, or data transformation tasks, these tools will prove invaluable in writing optimized and powerful SQL queries.

CHAPTER 18

VIEWS

Views are an important feature in SQL that allow you to create **virtual tables** based on the result set of a query. They don't store data themselves but instead store a SQL query that can be executed whenever you need to access the data. Understanding views and how they work is essential for writing more efficient, readable, and reusable SQL code.

In this chapter, we'll cover what views are, their benefits and drawbacks, and how to create and manage views in your database.

What is a View? Creating Virtual Tables

A **view** in SQL is essentially a stored query that behaves like a table. It can contain a SELECT statement that pulls data from one or more tables and presents it in a format that can be queried just like a table. While views do not actually store data themselves, they provide a way to simplify complex queries by encapsulating them into a virtual table.

Syntax:

```sql
```

```sql
CREATE VIEW view_name AS
SELECT column1, column2, ...
FROM table_name
WHERE condition;
```

Example:

Imagine you want to create a view that retrieves all employees from a specific department with their full name and salary, which you will frequently use. Instead of repeating the same query multiple times, you can define a view for it.

sql

```sql
CREATE VIEW employee_salaries AS
SELECT first_name || ' ' || last_name AS
full_name, department, salary
FROM employees
WHERE department = 'Sales';
```

Now, instead of writing the SELECT query each time, you can access the view employee_salaries as if it were a regular table:

sql

```sql
SELECT * FROM employee_salaries;
```

This will return a list of full names, departments, and salaries of employees in the "Sales" department.

Benefits and Drawbacks of Views: When and Why to Use Them

Views provide a range of benefits, but like any tool, they come with some limitations. Let's look at both sides.

Benefits of Views:

1. **Simplifying Complex Queries:** Views allow you to create a layer of abstraction, simplifying complex SQL queries. You can encapsulate complicated logic and join operations into a view, so users and developers can query it without worrying about the complexity.

    o **Example:** A view can hide complex joins, calculations, or subqueries. Users only need to interact with the view as if it were a simple table.

2. **Data Security:** Views can be used to limit access to specific columns or rows of a table, ensuring sensitive data is not exposed. By restricting access to certain parts of the database, you can enforce more secure interactions with the database.

    o **Example:** A view might only show non-sensitive employee information, such as name and department, but not salary or personal data.

3. **Reusability and Maintainability:** Once a view is created, it can be reused in multiple queries, ensuring consistency and reducing the need to repeat SQL code. If

the underlying query logic needs to change, you only need to update the view, rather than modifying every query that uses it.

4. **Improved Readability:** By abstracting away complex joins and logic, views improve the readability and maintainability of your SQL code.

Drawbacks of Views:

1. **Performance Issues:** Since views are essentially stored queries, every time you query a view, the underlying query must be executed. For complex views with many joins or large datasets, this can lead to performance issues, especially if the view is queried frequently.

   o **Solution:** Use views thoughtfully and monitor performance. In some cases, creating indexes or materialized views (explained later) can help.

2. **No Indexing:** You cannot create indexes on views themselves, which can slow down performance for complex queries. Indexes must be created on the underlying tables.

3. **Limited Functionality:** While views are powerful, they are limited in functionality compared to tables. For instance, you can't directly insert, update, or delete data in a view (unless the view is simple and meets certain conditions, such as being based on a single table).

4. **Not Always Up-to-Date:** Since views don't store data but instead retrieve it dynamically from underlying tables, the data in a view will always reflect the current state of the underlying tables. However, if the underlying data changes frequently, performance could degrade if the view is complex.

Creating and Dropping Views

Creating a View:

To create a view, you simply use the CREATE VIEW statement, followed by the SQL query that defines the view. As shown earlier, the view definition is stored in the database, and you can access it later just like a table.

Syntax:

sql

```
CREATE VIEW view_name AS
SELECT column1, column2, ...
FROM table_name
WHERE condition;
```

You can also create a view that is more complex, involving multiple tables, joins, or aggregations.

181

Example:
sql

```
CREATE VIEW department_averages AS
SELECT department, AVG(salary) AS avg_salary
FROM employees
GROUP BY department;
```

This view returns the average salary for each department, and you can query it like a regular table:

sql

```
SELECT * FROM department_averages;
```

Dropping a View:

If you no longer need a view or want to remove it, you can use the DROP VIEW statement. Dropping a view does not affect the underlying data in the database; it only removes the view definition.

Syntax:
sql

```
DROP VIEW view_name;
```

Example:
sql

```
DROP VIEW department_averages;
```

Updating Data via Views

In general, you cannot directly modify data in a view, especially if the view is based on multiple tables or contains aggregate functions. However, in some cases, it is possible to update data through a view if it meets certain conditions (e.g., it is based on a single table, and no complex joins or aggregations are involved).

Example of an Updatable View:

If the view is based on a simple query, like pulling data from a single table, it may be updatable:

sql

```
CREATE VIEW active_employees AS
SELECT employee_id, employee_name
FROM employees
WHERE status = 'Active';

-- This view can be updated since it's based on
a single table
UPDATE active_employees
SET employee_name = 'John Doe'
WHERE employee_id = 1;
```

However, if you try to update a view that involves complex joins or aggregation, you will typically encounter an error. To make changes to data in such views, you must modify the underlying tables directly.

Conclusion

Views are an incredibly useful tool in SQL for abstracting complex queries, improving readability, and enhancing security by limiting access to certain data. While they come with some drawbacks, such as performance concerns and limitations on updates, their benefits in terms of simplifying query logic and promoting code reuse are undeniable.

In this chapter, we learned how to create, manage, and drop views, as well as when and why to use them. Views can significantly improve the maintainability and organization of your database, especially in large systems with complex relationships and data retrieval needs. However, it's essential to consider the performance implications and limitations when using views, and understand when it may be better to use other techniques, such as direct table queries or materialized views.

CHAPTER 19

STORED PROCEDURES

Stored procedures are like the "functions" of the database world. They let you save blocks of SQL code that you can call and reuse, rather than rewriting the same queries over and over again. This helps keep your code DRY (Don't Repeat Yourself), makes your applications more efficient, and reduces the chances of mistakes.

In this chapter, we'll cover what stored procedures are, how to create and manage them, and when they're actually worth using.

What Are Stored Procedures? Reusable SQL Code Blocks

A **stored procedure** is a named collection of SQL statements that's saved in the database. You can run it just like you would run a function in programming.

Think of it as precompiled SQL that lives on the database server. Once created, you (or any app connected to the DB) can call it with a single line and pass in parameters if needed.

185

Why they exist:

- Save time on repetitive tasks.
- Improve performance for frequently used logic.
- Enforce consistency in data operations.
- Separate business logic from application logic.

Basic Syntax (MySQL-style):

```sql

DELIMITER $$

CREATE PROCEDURE procedure_name (param1 INT,
param2 VARCHAR(100))
BEGIN
    -- SQL statements go here
    SELECT * FROM some_table WHERE id = param1;
END$$

DELIMITER ;
```

Once created, you can call the procedure with:

```sql

CALL procedure_name(5, 'some value');
```

Creating and Managing Stored Procedures

Creating a stored procedure varies slightly between database systems, but the general idea is the same. You define the name, list parameters (if any), and provide the SQL statements to run.

Step-by-step:

1. **Define the procedure name and parameters**
2. **Write your logic**
3. **Wrap it in BEGIN...END**
4. **Use DELIMITER if your DBMS requires it (MySQL does)**

Example: Simple Procedure with No Parameters

sql

```
DELIMITER //

CREATE PROCEDURE get_all_customers()
BEGIN
    SELECT * FROM customers;
END //

DELIMITER ;
```

Example: Procedure with Parameters

sql

```
DELIMITER //
```

187

```
CREATE        PROCEDURE        get_customer_by_id(IN
customer_id INT)
BEGIN
    SELECT  *  FROM  customers  WHERE  id  =
customer_id;
END //
```

```
DELIMITER ;
```

Calling the procedure:

```
sql
```

```
CALL get_customer_by_id(3);
```

Modifying a Procedure:

In some databases (like PostgreSQL), you have to drop and recreate the procedure to modify it. In MySQL, you also typically drop and re-create:

```
sql
```

```
DROP PROCEDURE IF EXISTS get_customer_by_id;
```

When to Use Stored Procedures for Efficiency

Stored procedures aren't always necessary, but in the right context, they're extremely useful. Let's break down a few cases where they shine:

✓Use them when:

- You need to run the same complex query multiple times (e.g., monthly reporting).
- You're performing multi-step transactions (e.g., update several tables, then log it).
- You want to hide business logic from the front-end or other teams.
- You're optimizing for performance by minimizing the number of calls between your app and the DB.

✗Avoid them when:

- You're dealing with very simple queries that don't benefit from reuse.
- You prefer to keep all logic in the application layer for portability.
- You need real-time dynamic SQL generation (which is possible but messy in procedures).

Real-World Use Case:

Imagine a logistics app. Every time a delivery is completed, you need to:

1. Update the delivery status.
2. Record the delivery timestamp.
3. Log the delivery in a history table.

189

4.   Trigger a stored procedure to send an email notification.

Rather than writing that in your app in four different SQL calls, you write one stored procedure that handles all of it inside the database:

sql

```
CREATE        PROCEDURE        complete_delivery(IN
delivery_id INT)
BEGIN
    UPDATE deliveries SET status = 'Completed',
completed_at = NOW() WHERE id = delivery_id;
    INSERT  INTO  delivery_log  (delivery_id,
action,   timestamp)   VALUES   (delivery_id,
'Completed', NOW());
    -- Add more steps if needed
END;
```

Then your app just calls:

sql

```
CALL complete_delivery(1007);
```

Other Considerations

- **Security:** Stored procedures can help control access. You can allow a user to execute a procedure without giving them direct access to the tables it modifies.

- **Error handling:** Many SQL systems let you use `DECLARE`, `HANDLER`, or `TRY/CATCH` blocks inside procedures.

- **Debugging:** Debugging stored procedures can be frustrating. Most tools don't give great error messages. Start simple, test often.

Summary

Stored procedures help you write once and reuse often. They're ideal when you're repeating complex SQL operations, working with transactions, or keeping database logic away from your main application. Like any tool, they're most helpful when used deliberately—not just for the sake of using them.

In the next chapter, we'll look at **Triggers**, which let you run SQL automatically when certain events happen inside your database— kind of like reactive SQL.

CHAPTER 20

TRIGGERS

Triggers are like event listeners in your database. They respond automatically to changes—whenever a specific event (INSERT, UPDATE, DELETE) happens on a table, the trigger fires and executes predefined SQL statements. They're powerful but also easy to misuse if you're not paying attention.

This chapter covers what triggers are, how to set them up, and when they actually make sense in a real-world database.

What is a Trigger?

A **trigger** is a piece of SQL code that runs **automatically** in response to an event happening to a table. You don't manually call a trigger—it just does its thing when the right conditions are met.

Events that can activate a trigger:

- `INSERT`: After new data is added
- `UPDATE`: When data is changed
- `DELETE`: When data is removed

Timing options:

- BEFORE: Trigger runs before the change happens
- AFTER: Trigger runs after the change happens

This makes triggers useful for:

- Validating or modifying data before it hits the table
- Automatically logging changes
- Enforcing business rules at the database level

Creating and Managing Triggers

Let's say you want to log every time a user is deleted. You could create an AFTER DELETE trigger that copies their info into a backup table before it's gone for good.

Example: MySQL syntax

```sql
sql

CREATE TRIGGER log_user_deletion
AFTER DELETE ON users
FOR EACH ROW
BEGIN
    INSERT INTO deleted_users_log (user_id,
deleted_at)
    VALUES (OLD.id, NOW());
```

193

```
END;
```

Explanation:

- FOR EACH ROW: The trigger runs for every affected row (not just once per statement).
- OLD: Refers to the row **before** it was deleted.
- NEW: Refers to the new row in case of INSERT or UPDATE.

Another example: Prevent certain updates
sql

```
CREATE TRIGGER prevent_price_drop
BEFORE UPDATE ON products
FOR EACH ROW
BEGIN
    IF NEW.price < OLD.price THEN
        SIGNAL SQLSTATE '45000' SET MESSAGE_TEXT
= 'Price reduction not allowed';
    END IF;
END;
```

Here, the trigger stops the update from happening if someone tries to lower the price.

Managing Triggers

Like other DB objects, you can list, drop, or disable triggers as needed.

List all triggers (MySQL):
sql

```
SHOW TRIGGERS;
```

Drop a trigger:
sql

```
DROP TRIGGER IF EXISTS log_user_deletion;
```

In PostgreSQL and SQL Server, syntax differs a bit, but the concepts are the same.

Use Cases for Triggers in Database Design

Triggers are useful in very specific scenarios—especially when you want something to happen automatically behind the scenes.

✅*Good use cases:*

- **Audit trails**: Automatically log who changed what and when.
- **Soft deletes**: Instead of deleting rows, you mark them as deleted.

- **Automatic updates**: Like updating a `last_modified` timestamp column.
- **Data validation**: Prevent incorrect values from being inserted/updated.
- **Synchronizing tables**: For example, mirroring records in a backup or archive table.

✗ *Situations to avoid:*

- Business logic that should live in your app, not the database.
- When triggers make debugging a nightmare.
- Overengineering—when a simple query or procedure would work better.

Real-World Scenario:

In an e-commerce app, every time an order is placed (`INSERT` into `orders`), you want to:

1. Deduct the item quantity from inventory.
2. Update a running sales total in another table.
3. Log the order to an audit table.

You could build three `AFTER INSERT` triggers on the `orders` table to handle each of these automatically, without needing to manage that logic in your application code.

Final Thoughts

Triggers are powerful, but they're not magic. Use them for automation and safety nets, not for hiding logic you'll forget exists later. Too many triggers can slow down your database and create unpredictable behavior if not handled carefully.

Next up, we'll go into **User Management and Security**—how to control who can access your data and what they can do with it.

CHAPTER 21

DATABASE SECURITY

You can write clean queries and build the most efficient tables in the world—but if your database isn't secure, you're sitting on a ticking time bomb. Data breaches, unauthorized access, and sloppy permissions can undo all your hard work in seconds.

This chapter gets into the real stuff: who gets access, how to stop attackers, and what to do with sensitive data so it's not just floating around in plain text.

User Privileges and Permissions: Who Gets to Touch What

Every user that connects to a database should only be able to do what they actually need to do—no more, no less. That's the baseline rule of database security: **least privilege**.

Common Roles and Permissions

Here's what you're typically controlling:

- SELECT: Can view data

198

- INSERT: Can add data
- UPDATE: Can change existing data
- DELETE: Can remove data
- CREATE, ALTER, DROP: Can change database structure
- EXECUTE: Can run stored procedures or functions

Example: MySQL user setup

sql

```sql
CREATE USER 'report_user'@'%' IDENTIFIED BY 'strongpassword';

GRANT SELECT ON sales_db.* TO 'report_user'@'%';
```

This gives report_user read-only access to all tables in sales_db, from any host.

Best practices:

- Never give full ALL PRIVILEGES access unless absolutely necessary.
- Separate read and write users.
- Rotate passwords regularly (yes, even for service accounts).
- Use role-based access if your DBMS supports it.

SQL Injection: Don't Let Hackers Write SQL for You

SQL injection happens when you let raw, user-supplied input go straight into a query. It's one of the oldest attacks in the book—and it still works when developers get lazy.

The classic example:

```sql
```

```sql
SELECT * FROM users WHERE username = 'admin' AND
password = 'password';
```

If the input isn't sanitized, a malicious user could enter:

```vbnet
```

```
' OR 1=1 --
```

Which turns your query into:

```sql
```

```sql
SELECT * FROM users WHERE username = '' OR 1=1 -
-' AND password = 'password';
```

That `1=1` always returns true, and the `--` comments out the rest. Boom—access granted.

How to prevent SQL injection:

1. **Use prepared statements** / parameterized queries.
    o   In Python with SQLite:

    ```python
    cursor.execute("SELECT * FROM users
    WHERE username = ? AND password = ?",
    (user, pw))
    ```

2. **Never build queries by string concatenation.**
3. **Escape all user input** if you absolutely have to build raw SQL (not recommended).
4. **Use ORM libraries** (e.g., SQLAlchemy, Sequelize) that abstract queries safely.

Encryption and Data Masking: Keep It Hidden

If someone gets into your database, you don't want them reading sensitive data like it's an open book.

Encryption at Rest

This protects your data while it's sitting in storage (disk, SSD, backups, etc.).

- Your DBMS or hosting provider should support this by default.
- You can also use file-level encryption (like BitLocker or LUKS) for on-prem servers.

Encryption in Transit

This protects data being transmitted over the network.

- Always use SSL/TLS when connecting to a database remotely.
- Some databases let you force encrypted connections.

Column-level encryption

Encrypt specific sensitive fields, like social security numbers or credit card details.

- You'll often need to encrypt/decrypt in the application layer.
- Be mindful of performance—encryption isn't cheap.

Data Masking

Instead of showing full data, you show only part of it—great for dev environments or read-only dashboards.

Example:

```sql
SELECT CONCAT(SUBSTRING(ssn, 1, 3), '-XX-XXXX')
AS masked_ssn FROM employees;
```

Final Tips

- Monitor everything: Keep logs of access, queries, errors, and failed logins.
- Backups aren't security, but losing them *is* a disaster. Secure and encrypt those too.
- Patch your DBMS regularly—don't get owned because you skipped a security update.

Summary

Security isn't optional. If you're working with databases, you're responsible for guarding them. From managing user permissions, to preventing injection attacks, to encrypting sensitive data— every step matters. You don't need to go full cybersecurity engineer, but you can't ignore it either.

Next up, we'll cover **Database Backups and Recovery**—because sooner or later, something will go wrong, and you'll need a plan that doesn't involve panicking.

CHAPTER 22

BACKUPS AND RESTORES

Even the most carefully designed databases can experience unexpected issues: hardware failures, human errors, software bugs, or even malicious attacks. The difference between a minor hiccup and a major disaster is having a robust **backup and restore** strategy in place. Without backups, you're gambling with your data.

In this chapter, we'll dive into how to back up your databases, the steps to restore them when disaster strikes, and how to automate the entire process to minimize risks.

Backing Up Databases: Methods for Ensuring Data Safety

A database backup is essentially a snapshot of your data at a given point in time. Having regular backups can save you from catastrophic data loss, but it's crucial to understand different backup methods to choose the one that best fits your needs.

Types of Database Backups:

1. **Full Backups**:
    o   A complete copy of all data in the database.
    o   Time-consuming and storage-heavy, but reliable.
    o   Recommended for initial backups or periodic full backups.

    Example (MySQL):

    ```bash
    mysqldump -u root -p mydatabase > mydatabase_backup.sql
    ```

2. **Incremental Backups**:
    o   Only changes made since the last backup are stored. It's more efficient in terms of storage and time, but requires a previous full backup.
    o   Often used with full backups to save space.

    Example (MySQL):

    ```bash
    mysqlbackup --incremental --backup-dir=/path/to/incremental_backup backup
    ```

3. **Differential Backups**:

205

- Similar to incremental backups, but they save all changes since the last full backup, rather than since the last incremental one.
- These are a good compromise between full and incremental backups.

4. **Point-in-Time Backups**:
  - Captures the state of a database at a specific moment. Often used in systems that need to ensure transactions are captured precisely, such as financial or healthcare databases.
  - Achieved with transaction logs or binary logs that track every change to the database.

Example (PostgreSQL):

bash

```
pg_basebackup -D /path/to/backup -Ft -z -P
```

Best Practices for Backups:

- **Offsite backups**: Store backups in a different physical location (or in the cloud) to prevent data loss in case of a local disaster.
- **Regular schedules**: Set up daily, weekly, or monthly backups depending on how often your data changes.

- **Test your backups**: A backup that can't be restored is useless. Periodically test restoring your backups to make sure they're working.
- **Versioning**: Keep multiple versions of backups so you can recover from any point, not just the last one.
- **Compression**: Consider compressing backups to save space, especially for large databases.

Restoring Databases: Steps to Recover Data in Case of Failure

When disaster strikes, it's not enough to just have backups—you need to know how to restore your data quickly and correctly. Restoring a database involves bringing your data back to the state it was in during the backup.

Full Backup Restore:

1. **MySQL**:

   ```
   bash

   mysql   -u   root   -p   mydatabase   <
   mydatabase_backup.sql
   ```

2. **PostgreSQL**:

207

```bash
pg_restore      -C      -d      postgres
/path/to/backup.dump
```

Incremental and Differential Restore:

For incremental or differential backups, restoring requires more than one backup set.

- Restore the full backup first.
- Apply the incremental or differential backups in order, from the last full backup to the most recent incremental one.

Point-in-Time Recovery:

If you're using point-in-time recovery, you'll need to apply the transaction logs to bring the database to a precise point.

- In MySQL, you can use `mysqlbinlog` to apply binary logs.
- In PostgreSQL, you'd use WAL (Write-Ahead Log) files to roll forward to a specific point.

Verifying Restoration:

After restoring a backup, always verify that the data is intact and accurate.

- Check the integrity of the database.
- Run application queries to ensure everything is functioning properly.

Automating Backups: Scheduling and Tools to Manage Backups

Backups should be set up to run **automatically** so that you're never relying on someone to remember to do it manually. Automation helps ensure your backup strategy is consistent and error-free.

Scheduling Backups:

You can use system scheduling tools like **cron** (Linux) or **Task Scheduler** (Windows) to automate backup processes.

Example with cron (Linux): To schedule a daily backup at 2 AM:

```bash
0 2 * * * mysqldump -u root -p mydatabase > /path/to/backups/mydatabase_$(date +\%F).sql
```

Backup Tools:

There are many third-party tools available to help manage backups, including:

- **MySQL Workbench**: Built-in backup tools for MySQL, with scheduling options.
- **pgBackRest**: A reliable backup solution for PostgreSQL with compression and encryption.
- **Barman**: A backup and recovery manager for PostgreSQL.
- **AWS RDS**: For cloud-hosted databases, services like AWS RDS handle automated backups and snapshots.

Cloud Backups:

Using cloud platforms (e.g., **AWS**, **Google Cloud**, **Azure**) can simplify backup management:

- **Automated snapshot** features that take full backups of the database.
- **Offsite storage** to prevent local disasters from affecting your data.
- **Version control** and easy retrieval of historical backups.

Best Practices for Backup and Recovery

- **Use redundancy**: Backup your backups. For example, store copies in multiple locations (e.g., on-site and in the cloud).
- **Set retention policies**: Keep backups only for as long as necessary to avoid unnecessary storage costs. Automate the deletion of old backups.
- **Monitor backup processes**: Ensure backups are running as expected with notifications for failures.
- **Document your restore process**: Have a clear, documented process for restoring from backups. This way, in the event of a failure, your team can act quickly.
- **Minimize downtime**: For high-availability systems, consider setting up **replication** to keep a live copy of the database in sync and ready to take over in case of failure.

Summary

In a world where data is central to everything, backups and restores aren't optional—they're a lifeline. It's essential to understand the different types of backups, how to restore data, and how to automate the entire process to ensure your database is safe and recoverable. A solid backup strategy can be the difference between a minor inconvenience and a major data disaster.

In the next chapter, we'll discuss **Database Optimization and Tuning**, to ensure your database performs efficiently even as it scales.

CHAPTER 23

OPTIMIZING SQL QUERIES

As your database grows, queries that once ran quickly can start to lag. Slow queries not only hurt user experience but can also lead to resource inefficiencies, causing slowdowns for the entire system. That's why optimizing SQL queries is crucial.

This chapter will walk you through how to identify performance bottlenecks, optimize slow queries, and leverage tools like **EXPLAIN plans**, **indexes**, and **query caching** to speed things up.

Using EXPLAIN Plans: How to Analyze Query Performance

EXPLAIN is your first tool in debugging a slow query. It tells you how the SQL engine plans to execute your query, so you can see where the inefficiencies are.

What EXPLAIN Shows:

- **Table scans**: If a query is scanning the whole table instead of using an index, that's a sign of inefficiency.

213

- **Joins**: Whether the joins are using indexes or doing a full table scan.
- **Indexes used**: If the query is using indexes efficiently or not at all.
- **Sort operations**: Whether the database is sorting large result sets in memory.

Example: Using EXPLAIN in MySQL

sql

```
EXPLAIN SELECT name, age FROM users WHERE age >
25;
```

This will output a table that shows the type of scan being used, indexes, and more. Here's an example of a typical output:

pgsql

```
+----+-------------+--------+-------+----------
--------+---------+---------+------+--------+--
--------------------+
| id | select_type | table  | type  |
possible_keys    | key     | key_len | ref  |
rows | Extra                |
+----+-------------+--------+-------+----------
--------+---------+---------+------+--------+--
--------------------+
```

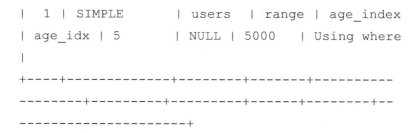

```
|  1 | SIMPLE     | users  | range | age_index
| age_idx | 5     | NULL | 5000   | Using where
|
+----+------------+--------+-------+----------
--------+---------+---------+------+--------+--
-------------------+
```

- **type**: In this example, `range` indicates that an index is being used efficiently.
- **key**: Shows which index is being used (`age_idx`).
- **rows**: Indicates how many rows will be examined. Fewer rows are better.

Interpreting EXPLAIN Output:

- **ALL**: Full table scan. This is slow for large tables.
- **index**: Index scan, good.
- **range**: Index range scan, better than a full table scan.
- **ref**: Efficient join condition using an indexed column.

If EXPLAIN shows a full table scan (`ALL`), that's a sign that you may need to optimize the query with better indexes or a different approach.

Optimizing Joins and Subqueries

215

Joins and subqueries are often the culprits in slow queries. Here are some tips to optimize their performance:

1. Use Proper Join Types

- **INNER JOIN**: Only returns rows that have matching values in both tables. Use this when you need to combine data from two related tables.
- **LEFT JOIN**: Returns all rows from the left table and matching rows from the right table. Use this when you need all rows from one table, even if no match exists in the other table.

Joins can be slow if there's no proper indexing on the join column, so always ensure that columns used in JOIN conditions are indexed.

Example:

sql

```
SELECT u.name, o.order_date
FROM users u
INNER JOIN orders o ON u.id = o.user_id
WHERE o.order_date > '2023-01-01';
```

- The **INNER JOIN** is often faster than a **LEFT JOIN** because it eliminates unmatched rows upfront.

2. Subqueries vs. Joins

Sometimes, subqueries are slower than joins. This is because the database may need to execute the subquery for every row in the outer query.

Bad Subquery Example:

sql

```
SELECT name
FROM users
WHERE id IN (SELECT user_id FROM orders WHERE
order_date > '2023-01-01');
```

Here, the subquery runs for each user, potentially causing inefficiency. Rewriting this as a join is often more efficient:

Better Query with JOIN:

sql

```
SELECT DISTINCT u.name
FROM users u
JOIN orders o ON u.id = o.user_id
WHERE o.order_date > '2023-01-01';
```

3. Use EXISTS for Subqueries

When using subqueries, **EXISTS** is often more efficient than **IN**, especially with larger data sets. EXISTS checks for the existence of rows, while IN compares all the values.

```sql
sql

SELECT name
FROM users u
WHERE EXISTS (SELECT 1 FROM orders o WHERE
o.user_id = u.id AND o.order_date > '2023-01-
01');
```

4. Avoid N+1 Queries

An N+1 query problem occurs when a query fetches a list of items and then runs additional queries for each item individually. This can cause an explosion in the number of queries being executed. You can solve this by using a **JOIN** instead of multiple queries.

Indexes and Query Caching: Leveraging These to Speed Up Performance

Indexes and query caching are two of the most powerful tools in your arsenal for speeding up queries.

1. Indexing for Speed

Indexes are like tables of contents for your database. They help the database find the rows you're looking for without scanning the entire table.

- **When to index**: Index columns that are frequently used in **WHERE, JOIN,** and **ORDER BY** clauses.
- **Avoid over-indexing**: Too many indexes can actually slow down INSERT, UPDATE, and DELETE operations because the indexes must also be updated.

Example of Creating an Index:
sql

```
CREATE INDEX idx_user_age ON users(age);
```

2. Query Caching

Many database systems support query caching, which stores the result of a query in memory so that it doesn't have to be recalculated each time it's executed. However, caching is effective only for **read-heavy** workloads and queries that don't change often.

- **MySQL** has query caching, but it's disabled by default in modern versions.
- **PostgreSQL** doesn't have built-in query caching, but caching can be implemented at the application level.

219

You can also consider using a caching layer like **Redis** or **Memcached** to store results from expensive queries for faster access.

Example:
sql

```
SELECT * FROM products WHERE category = 'electronics';
```

If this query is frequently run, you can cache the result and fetch it from memory instead of querying the database each time.

3. Composite Indexes

If your queries use multiple columns in the WHERE clause, consider creating a composite index. A composite index is an index on multiple columns.

sql

```
CREATE INDEX idx_user_name_age ON users(name, age);
```

This index is particularly useful for queries that filter on both name and age.

4. Analyzing Index Usage

Not all indexes are created equal. Use tools like **EXPLAIN** to ensure that your indexes are being utilized effectively. If they're not, it may be a sign you need to rethink your indexing strategy.

Best Practices for Query Optimization:

1. **Avoid SELECT ***: Only select the columns you actually need. Selecting all columns can slow things down, especially with large tables.

2. **Minimize DISTINCT**: Use DISTINCT only when absolutely necessary, as it can be resource-intensive.

3. **Limit Your Result Set**: Use LIMIT or TOP to restrict the number of rows returned, especially in development or testing environments.

4. **Optimize Joins**: Choose the correct type of join, and ensure that the join condition uses indexed columns.

5. **Analyze Query Performance Regularly**: Use tools like **EXPLAIN, slow query logs**, and **performance monitoring tools** to keep your queries in check as your database grows.

Summary

Optimizing SQL queries is an ongoing process, and there's always room to improve performance. By analyzing query plans with **EXPLAIN**, optimizing **joins and subqueries**, and leveraging **indexes** and **query caching**, you can dramatically improve the efficiency of your database. As your system grows, performance tuning should be part of your regular maintenance routine.

In the next chapter, we'll cover **Database Scaling and Sharding**, discussing how to scale your database to handle growing amounts of data and traffic.

CHAPTER 24

DATABASE DESIGN PRINCIPLES

Database design is the blueprint for how your data is stored, structured, and accessed. The design choices you make will affect how easy it is to maintain, scale, and query your database. A well-designed database can save you time and resources in the long run, whereas a poor design can lead to performance issues, data inconsistencies, and unnecessary complexity.

In this chapter, we'll walk through the essential database design principles, including how to visualize your structure using **ER diagrams**, how to define relationships using **primary** and **foreign keys**, and how to plan for growth.

ER Diagrams: Visualizing Database Structure

Entity-Relationship (ER) diagrams are a visual tool used to map out the structure of your database. They help you conceptualize how the tables in your database relate to one another and allow you to communicate your design to stakeholders or team members.

223

What is an ER Diagram?

An ER diagram represents entities (tables) in a database and the relationships between them. Entities are represented as boxes, while relationships are shown as lines connecting the boxes. Attributes, or columns, are usually listed inside each entity box.

- **Entities**: Tables or objects (e.g., `users`, `orders`).
- **Attributes**: Columns inside tables (e.g., `user_id`, `user_name`).
- **Relationships**: Connections between tables (e.g., a user placing an order).

Example of an ER Diagram:

Imagine a simple e-commerce database with two tables: `users` and `orders`. The relationship is that one user can place many orders.

pgsql

```
+-----------+         +-----------+
|   Users   |         |  Orders   |
+-----------+         +-----------+
| user_id   |----->| order_id  |
| name      |         | user_id   |
| email     |         | order_date|
+-----------+         +-----------+
```

- The **Users** table has a `user_id` as a primary key.
- The **Orders** table has a `user_id` as a foreign key, linking it to the `Users` table.

Why Use ER Diagrams?

- **Clarity**: They provide a clear overview of how data is structured and related.
- **Collaboration**: They make it easier to communicate your database design to others, especially in a team setting.
- **Efficiency**: They help identify potential issues with the structure early on, like missing relationships or unnecessary redundancies.

Choosing Primary Keys and Foreign Keys: Best Practices for Defining Relationships

Primary Keys

A **primary key** is a column or set of columns that uniquely identifies each row in a table. The primary key must be unique and not NULL.

Best Practices for Primary Keys:

1. **Uniqueness**: The primary key must uniquely identify each row.
2. **Simplicity**: Use a single column whenever possible (e.g., `user_id`).
3. **Consistency**: Avoid using data that might change (e.g., email addresses) as a primary key.
4. **Use Surrogate Keys**: Use auto-incrementing integers or GUIDs for primary keys instead of natural keys, which are more likely to change.

Foreign Keys

A **foreign key** is a column or set of columns in one table that refers to the primary key of another table. Foreign keys define the relationship between tables and enforce referential integrity.

Best Practices for Foreign Keys:

1. **Establish Relationships**: Foreign keys help maintain the relationship between related tables.
2. **Referential Integrity**: The foreign key ensures that any data inserted into the foreign key column exists in the referenced table's primary key column.

3. **Cascading Updates and Deletes**: When records in the parent table are updated or deleted, cascading actions can be triggered on the child table to maintain integrity.

Example of Primary and Foreign Keys:

Consider an e-commerce database with `orders` and `customers`. Here, `order_id` is the primary key in `orders`, while `customer_id` is a foreign key in the `orders` table referring to the `customer_id` in the `customers` table.

sql

```
CREATE TABLE customers (
    customer_id INT AUTO_INCREMENT PRIMARY KEY,
    name VARCHAR(255),
    email VARCHAR(255) UNIQUE
);

CREATE TABLE orders (
    order_id INT AUTO_INCREMENT PRIMARY KEY,
    customer_id INT,
    order_date DATE,
    FOREIGN   KEY   (customer_id)   REFERENCES
customers(customer_id)
);
```

- **customer_id** in the `orders` table is a foreign key linking it to the `customers` table.

227

Designing for Scale: Planning for Future Database Growth

As your application grows, so will your data. Planning for scale is essential to ensure that your database can handle increased traffic and data volume over time without performance degradation.

1. Normalize Data to Reduce Redundancy

Data **normalization** involves organizing your database to minimize redundancy and improve data integrity. This is typically done by splitting data into multiple related tables. However, normalization can sometimes lead to performance issues due to the need for frequent joins. In some cases, denormalization may be necessary for performance reasons.

2. Choose Scalable Database Systems

Not all database systems are built to scale in the same way. While **MySQL** or **PostgreSQL** are popular relational databases, they can struggle with horizontal scaling (across multiple servers) when the database becomes too large. Consider distributed databases or cloud-based databases like **Google BigQuery** or **Amazon Aurora** if scalability is a concern.

3. Indexing and Partitioning

As your database grows, indexing becomes more important. In addition to creating indexes on frequently queried columns, you may want to use **partitioning**, which splits large tables into smaller, more manageable pieces based on certain criteria (e.g., range of dates or geographic location).

4. Replication and Sharding

For large-scale applications, **replication** (creating copies of your database on different servers) and **sharding** (splitting your database into smaller pieces, or shards, each hosted on a different server) are strategies to distribute load and improve performance.

5. Data Archiving and Purging

As the volume of data grows, it's important to periodically archive or purge old data that is no longer necessary for daily operations. This helps keep the active database lean and fast.

6. Database Monitoring and Optimization

As your database expands, continuous monitoring and optimization become more crucial. Use tools to track query performance, database load, and storage usage. Regularly analyze **slow queries** and optimize them to ensure your database can handle increasing traffic and data size efficiently.

Summary

Proper database design is foundational for the efficiency, scalability, and maintainability of your system. By visualizing your structure with **ER diagrams**, carefully selecting **primary and foreign keys**, and planning for future growth, you set your database up for success.

In the next chapter, we'll look at **Database Scaling and Sharding**, where we'll dive deeper into how to manage large-scale databases and distribute data across multiple systems.

CHAPTER 25

ADVANCED SQL CONCEPTS

As you progress in your SQL journey, there are certain advanced techniques that can help you handle complex data retrieval, improve query performance, and better organize large datasets. In this chapter, we will explore three essential advanced SQL concepts: **Recursive Queries**, **Full-Text Search**, and **Partitioning**. Mastering these topics will take your SQL skills to the next level and equip you to handle more sophisticated database challenges.

Recursive Queries: Using Recursive CTEs (Common Table Expressions)

Recursive queries are a powerful way to work with hierarchical or tree-structured data, such as organizational charts, file directories, or comment threads in a social media platform. Recursive **Common Table Expressions (CTEs)** allow you to write queries that refer to themselves, enabling you to retrieve data that is related in a recursive fashion.

What is a Recursive CTE?

A **Recursive CTE** is a temporary result set defined within the execution scope of a single query. It is composed of two parts:

1. **Base Case**: This part defines the starting point for the recursion (the simplest form of the query).
2. **Recursive Case**: This part references the CTE itself and allows it to repeatedly execute until the result set is complete.

Example of a Recursive Query:

Consider a table `employees` that stores employee data and includes a `manager_id` field to indicate each employee's manager. To retrieve the hierarchy of employees and their managers, you can use a recursive CTE.

sql

```
WITH RECURSIVE EmployeeHierarchy AS (
    -- Base case: Start with the top-level
employees (those with no manager)
    SELECT employee_id, name, manager_id
    FROM employees
    WHERE manager_id IS NULL


    UNION ALL
```

```
    -- Recursive case: Join the employees with
their managers
    SELECT e.employee_id, e.name, e.manager_id
    FROM employees e
    INNER JOIN EmployeeHierarchy eh ON
e.manager_id = eh.employee_id
)
SELECT * FROM EmployeeHierarchy;
```

- The **base case** selects employees who do not have a manager (`manager_id IS NULL`).
- The **recursive case** joins the `employees` table with the `EmployeeHierarchy` CTE, fetching each employee's manager and continuing this process until the entire hierarchy is retrieved.

When to Use Recursive Queries:

- Hierarchical data structures (e.g., organizational charts, category trees).
- Data where each item has a relationship to a previous or next item, such as a list of parts that make up a product or nested comments in a forum.

Full-Text Search: Setting Up and Using Full-Text Search Indexes

233

Full-text search is a feature that allows you to perform advanced searches on text-based columns in your database, such as searching for words or phrases within a large body of text. It is particularly useful for applications that need to handle search functionality, like content management systems, blogs, and e-commerce sites.

What is Full-Text Search?

Full-text search indexes allow for faster and more efficient searching of large amounts of text data. Rather than searching through text line by line, a full-text index creates a special data structure that indexes the words within the text, enabling faster search queries based on text patterns, word proximity, and relevance.

Setting Up Full-Text Search:

MySQL Example:

To enable full-text search in MySQL, you need to create a full-text index on the text column you want to search.

```sql
CREATE TABLE articles (
    article_id INT AUTO_INCREMENT PRIMARY KEY,
    title VARCHAR(255),
    content TEXT,
```

```
    FULLTEXT (title, content)
);
```

Now, you can perform full-text searches using the MATCH and AGAINST syntax:

sql

```
SELECT article_id, title
FROM articles
WHERE MATCH (title, content) AGAINST ('"database
design"');
```

This query searches the title and content columns for the phrase "database design". Full-text search also supports **boolean search** (using operators like +, -, * for wildcards, etc.), as well as **natural language searching**.

When to Use Full-Text Search:

- Searching for specific words or phrases within large text fields.
- Implementing search functionality for articles, blogs, or product descriptions.
- Searching over multiple columns, such as titles and content, in a single query.

Partitioning: Splitting Large Tables into Smaller, Manageable Pieces

As databases grow in size, performance can degrade when handling large tables with millions of rows. **Partitioning** is a technique used to split large tables into smaller, more manageable pieces (partitions) based on specific criteria, such as ranges of values or hash-based distributions. This helps to improve query performance, backup times, and maintenance efficiency.

What is Partitioning?

Partitioning allows you to divide a single large table into multiple smaller, more manageable parts. Each part, or partition, is stored separately, but it's still considered one logical table. You can partition tables based on various criteria, including:

- **Range Partitioning**: Partition data based on a range of values (e.g., date ranges).
- **List Partitioning**: Partition data based on specific values (e.g., region or category).
- **Hash Partitioning**: Partition data randomly or based on a hash value.
- **Key Partitioning**: Similar to hash partitioning but based on a key value.

Example of Partitioning in MySQL:

Let's say you have a `sales` table and want to partition it by year.

sql

```
CREATE TABLE sales (
    sale_id INT,
    sale_date DATE,
    amount DECIMAL(10, 2)
)
PARTITION BY RANGE (YEAR(sale_date)) (
    PARTITION p2019 VALUES LESS THAN (2020),
    PARTITION p2020 VALUES LESS THAN (2021),
    PARTITION p2021 VALUES LESS THAN (2022)
);
```

This query partitions the `sales` table into three partitions based on the year of the `sale_date`.

When to Use Partitioning:

- Tables with a large volume of data that are growing quickly (e.g., transaction logs, user activity logs).
- When querying specific subsets of data that can be isolated by range (e.g., queries by date range).
- To speed up read operations by limiting the number of rows scanned.

Benefits of Partitioning:

- **Improved Performance**: Queries targeting specific partitions can run faster since fewer rows need to be scanned.
- **Better Maintenance**: Partitioning can simplify data management tasks like backups, archiving, and purging old data.
- **Optimized Storage**: Partitioning can lead to more efficient storage by grouping related data together.

Summary

In this chapter, we have explored advanced SQL concepts that can significantly enhance your database management and querying abilities:

- **Recursive Queries** help you navigate hierarchical data and relationships within your database.
- **Full-Text Search** enables efficient searching of text-heavy data, making it ideal for applications with search functionality.
- **Partitioning** allows you to split large tables into smaller, more manageable units, improving performance and simplifying maintenance.

Mastering these advanced SQL concepts will help you design more sophisticated, scalable databases and optimize your SQL queries for better performance. In the next chapter, we'll focus on **Database Tuning and Optimization**, where we will delve into query optimization techniques, execution plans, and best practices for maintaining a healthy, high-performance database.

CHAPTER 26

SQL IN THE REAL WORLD

SQL is not just an abstract language for managing databases; it is a critical tool that powers the data infrastructure of businesses and applications all over the world. From e-commerce platforms to social media networks, SQL enables organizations to manage, retrieve, and analyze vast amounts of data efficiently. In this chapter, we will look at **real-world case studies** of SQL in action, explore how **SQL contributes to data analytics**, and discuss the integration of SQL with other technologies to build powerful, scalable applications.

Case Studies: Real-Life Examples of SQL in Action

Understanding how SQL is applied in real-world scenarios can give you deeper insights into its capabilities and practical applications. Below are some example case studies from different industries to showcase how SQL is utilized.

E-Commerce Databases

In an e-commerce platform, databases store information about products, customers, orders, payment methods, and shipping details. A SQL database powers the entire backend by efficiently querying large datasets to fetch relevant information when a user searches for a product, places an order, or checks their order status.

Example: Imagine a user searching for a specific product. An SQL query might look like this:

```sql
sql

SELECT product_name, price, stock_quantity
FROM products
WHERE category = 'electronics' AND price BETWEEN
100 AND 500
ORDER BY price DESC;
```

This query would fetch a list of electronic products within a price range, ordered by price. On the backend, SQL is used to process complex queries that join several tables (e.g., customers, orders, inventory) to give accurate, up-to-date information on product availability, customer preferences, and order status.

241

Social Media Platforms

Social media platforms like Facebook, Twitter, and Instagram rely heavily on SQL to manage user data, posts, interactions, and media. For example, retrieving a user's timeline or a list of friends involves running SQL queries on a large set of interconnected tables that store users' information, posts, comments, likes, and shares.

Example: Consider retrieving the posts of a user's friends (assuming a `friends` table and a `posts` table):

sql

```
SELECT          posts.post_id,          posts.content,
posts.timestamp
FROM posts
JOIN friends ON posts.user_id = friends.friend_id
WHERE friends.user_id = 12345
ORDER BY posts.timestamp DESC;
```

This query combines data from the `posts` and `friends` tables, displaying the posts from a user's friends, ordered by the most recent.

Healthcare Databases

In healthcare, SQL is used to manage patient records, prescriptions, diagnoses, and hospital scheduling systems. Given the sensitivity and complexity of healthcare data, SQL helps ensure data integrity, privacy, and security while providing fast access to relevant medical information.

Example: To find all prescriptions given to a particular patient, a SQL query could look like:

sql

```
SELECT prescription_id, medication_name, dosage,
date_prescribed
FROM prescriptions
WHERE patient_id = 98765;
```

In this case, SQL helps to quickly pull up all medication details associated with a given patient ID from the `prescriptions` table.

SQL and Data Analytics: SQL's Role in Data Science and Business Intelligence

SQL plays a critical role in the field of **data analytics**, **data science**, and **business intelligence** (BI). Whether you are querying a database for historical sales data or analyzing user behavior trends, SQL is often the starting point for gathering and analyzing data.

Extracting and Analyzing Data

Data scientists use SQL to extract raw data from relational databases, transform it into a usable format, and load it into analytical tools like Python, R, or Excel for further analysis. SQL's ability to perform powerful aggregations, filtering, and sorting makes it an ideal tool for quickly analyzing large datasets.

Example: A sales manager might want to know the total revenue for each region, grouped by year. Here's a sample SQL query for that:

sql

```
SELECT    region,    YEAR(sale_date)    AS    year,
SUM(amount) AS total_revenue
FROM sales
GROUP BY region, year
ORDER BY year;
```

This query aggregates the sales data by region and year, returning the total revenue for each region across different years. Such insights are valuable for business forecasting and decision-making.

SQL for Reporting and Dashboards

SQL is also commonly used in **business intelligence (BI)** tools like Tableau, Power BI, or Looker. These tools rely on SQL to retrieve data, which is then presented as visualizations and reports to help businesses track key performance indicators (KPIs), sales figures, and operational performance.

For example, in a dashboard that tracks monthly sales figures, a SQL query might pull the data that updates automatically to reflect the most recent sales:

```sql
sql

SELECT MONTH(sale_date) AS month, SUM(amount) AS monthly_sales
FROM sales
WHERE sale_date BETWEEN '2024-01-01' AND '2024-12-31'
GROUP BY month
ORDER BY month;
```

This query fetches the total sales amount for each month in 2024, which can then be visualized as a line graph or bar chart in a BI dashboard.

Integrating SQL with Other Technologies

SQL databases don't operate in isolation. They are typically integrated with other technologies to form the backbone of modern web applications, enterprise systems, and data-driven services.

SQL with Web Applications

When developing a web application (such as an e-commerce store, a blog platform, or a social network), SQL databases are used to store and retrieve data like user accounts, product listings, comments, etc. Web developers often use backend languages like PHP, Python, Ruby, or JavaScript (Node.js) to interact with SQL databases and serve dynamic content to users.

Example: In a Python-based web application using **Flask** or **Django**, you might interact with an SQL database as follows:

```python

import sqlite3

# Connect to database
conn = sqlite3.connect('database.db')
cursor = conn.cursor()

# Execute SQL query to fetch products
cursor.execute("SELECT product_name, price FROM products WHERE category = 'electronics'")
products = cursor.fetchall()

# Process the results
```

```
for product in products:
    print(product)
```

```
conn.close()
```

In this example, SQL is used to retrieve product data from a database, which can then be rendered in the web application's frontend.

SQL with APIs

SQL databases are also commonly integrated with **APIs** (Application Programming Interfaces). APIs allow external systems to interact with databases, enabling functionalities such as retrieving user profiles, adding orders, or fetching historical data.

For instance, an **e-commerce API** might allow users to view product listings or add items to their cart via HTTP requests. Behind the scenes, SQL queries are used to interact with the database and serve the appropriate data.

Example: When a user adds a product to their cart, an API endpoint might execute the following SQL query to update the cart:

```
sql
```

```
INSERT INTO shopping_cart (user_id, product_id,
quantity)
VALUES (12345, 67890, 1);
```

This SQL statement inserts the new cart item into the shopping_cart table, linking the product with the user's cart.

Summary

SQL's practical applications are wide-ranging and indispensable in the modern data landscape. In this chapter, we explored how SQL is used in:

- **Real-world case studies** like e-commerce platforms, social media networks, and healthcare systems, where SQL helps manage, query, and organize large datasets.
- **Data analytics**, where SQL is the backbone for extracting, processing, and analyzing data for business intelligence and decision-making.
- **Integrating SQL with other technologies**, such as web applications and APIs, to power dynamic, data-driven experiences.

Mastering SQL is not just about knowing how to write queries — it's about understanding its role in modern software and data architecture. Whether you're working in e-commerce, data science, or web development, SQL remains a cornerstone of data management and analysis.

In the next chapter, we will discuss **SQL in Cloud Databases**, exploring how cloud platforms like AWS, Azure, and Google Cloud are changing the way we use SQL to manage data at scale.

CHAPTER 27

THE FUTURE OF SQL AND DATABASE TECHNOLOGIES

SQL has been around for over four decades, and despite repeated predictions that newer technologies would replace it, SQL continues to evolve and maintain its relevance. But the data landscape isn't static. As applications get more complex, data volumes balloon, and systems move to the cloud, the way we think about databases—and SQL itself—is changing.

In this final chapter, we'll cover where SQL stands in the broader tech ecosystem, what alternatives like NoSQL bring to the table, how cloud services are changing database workflows, and which trends you should keep an eye on if you plan to stay current in the world of database tech.

NoSQL Databases: The Rise of Alternatives

Let's be honest—SQL isn't always the best fit for every problem.

While relational databases still dominate enterprise software and are excellent for structured, normalized data, there's a class of modern applications—think large-scale real-time analytics, flexible content management systems, and IoT platforms—where rigid schemas and traditional SQL just don't cut it.

Why NoSQL?

"NoSQL" doesn't mean "no to SQL." It means "not only SQL." These databases are built for scalability, flexibility, and high-speed operations across distributed systems. They support:

- **Key-Value Stores** (e.g., Redis): Excellent for caching and ultra-fast lookups.
- **Document Stores** (e.g., MongoDB): Ideal when you need flexible schemas.
- **Wide Column Stores** (e.g., Cassandra): Used in big data and real-time analytics.
- **Graph Databases** (e.g., Neo4j): Great for connected data like social networks or recommendation engines.

Each type comes with trade-offs, especially around consistency and querying capabilities, but their rise has forced SQL databases to innovate in return.

251

Cloud Databases: Rethinking Infrastructure

If you're building or managing a database today, chances are it lives in the cloud—or soon will.

What's Changing with the Cloud?

Cloud databases like **Amazon RDS**, **Google Cloud SQL**, **Azure SQL Database**, and **Firebase** are fundamentally changing how databases are deployed and maintained. The benefits are hard to ignore:

- **No more hardware provisioning**: No need to worry about servers or storage.
- **Automatic backups and updates**: Maintenance is mostly hands-off.
- **Built-in scalability**: Increase performance or storage with a few clicks.
- **Global availability**: Replicate across regions for low-latency access.

You're also seeing hybrid solutions emerge, like **Aurora Serverless,** which auto-scales based on demand, blending the best of both SQL and serverless design.

What This Means for SQL

SQL in the cloud often comes with additional features—automatic indexing suggestions, performance monitoring, AI-based query optimization, and more. But it also means developers need to understand billing models, latency implications, and how to design for multi-region consistency.

SQL Trends to Watch

SQL isn't frozen in time. New features, language extensions, and tool integrations are surfacing all the time. If you're building a career around databases, here are a few things you'll want to pay attention to.

1. JSON Support in SQL

More SQL engines now offer built-in support for JSON columns. This is a response to NoSQL's popularity, allowing developers to store semi-structured data without abandoning SQL entirely.

Example in PostgreSQL:

```sql
SELECT data->>'name' AS user_name
FROM users
```

253

```
WHERE data->>'role' = 'admin';
```

2. Graph and Geospatial Extensions

Modern SQL databases are starting to support graph queries (e.g., PostgreSQL with its `pgRouting` extension) and geospatial indexing (PostGIS). This means use cases like mapping apps or social networks can stick with SQL while adding more specialized querying power.

3. AI-Powered Query Optimization

AI and machine learning are starting to creep into SQL engines. Expect more intelligent query planners that can rewrite queries behind the scenes, suggest indexes, and adapt based on query patterns.

4. Better Tooling and UIs

Data is more accessible than ever with improved visualization tools, low-code database managers (like Retool or Supabase), and embedded SQL analytics tools. These are making SQL usable for analysts and business users who aren't engineers.

5. Serverless SQL Engines

Tools like BigQuery, Snowflake, and Amazon Athena let you write SQL directly against massive datasets stored in the cloud— without managing any infrastructure at all. You just pay for the queries you run. This changes how teams think about scaling analytics.

Where Does This Leave SQL Developers?

SQL is sticking around. If anything, it's becoming more versatile:

- You can write SQL against traditional relational databases.
- You can query semi-structured or streaming data.
- You can build APIs, dashboards, and real-time alerts off the back of SQL queries.
- You can integrate SQL with Python, R, and other modern languages for hybrid workflows.

And even if you're using NoSQL or serverless platforms, many are now adopting SQL-like languages (e.g., Google's BigQuery SQL, Cassandra's CQL) to make them more accessible.

The bottom line? Whether you're optimizing a classic OLTP system or building a distributed analytics pipeline, **understanding SQL is still a must-have skill**—and it's evolving in ways that make it more powerful than ever.

What's Next for You

Now that you've gone through the full spectrum—from basics to advanced techniques, design principles, and real-world applications—you're in a solid position to use SQL effectively, regardless of platform or use case.

Whether you're:

- Building your own projects
- Managing enterprise data
- Writing reports for business stakeholders
- Optimizing systems for performance
- Exploring data science
- Working in the cloud

SQL has the flexibility, power, and staying power to support it.

And if something newer comes along? You'll know exactly what SQL does well, where it falls short, and when to look elsewhere. That's the kind of perspective that separates beginners from professionals.

www.ingramcontent.com/pod-product-compliance
Lightning Source LLC
LaVergne TN
LVHW051443050326
832903LV00030BD/3209